I Knew

I was Different

MY PATH THROUGH TRAUMA

Rebecca Baker

This book is dedicated to

My Husband David, for getting me out of the attic and protecting me.

My kids, Harris, Hannah, Xander. You are my inspiration to become whole

So proud of the generational curses you broke.

I Love You

To all the victims of trauma and the survivors who chose to heal.

This is for you

Acknowledgements

For the unwavering belief and encouragement from my past and present therapists, JoAnn, Gina and Noel. Each of you provided the environment for my healing.

SWBC: My church where I can be me and I can feel my spirituality and not the religion.

To my Bible Study Group at a local church – Just thank you for your acceptance and love for me. I am learning a lot! Sherri, you're the best!

My Yoga Partner and friend: Ashley

To my agent and publishing company, Christian Mendez and Book-prime Publishing. I can't believe we did it!

My Olive Garden lunch partner: Stacy

DCFS and the foster care system

To my family-in-law – I'm sorry. I was very unhealthy and wanted a mom. Maybe some counter-transference happened.

To Bree – Thank you for my boy, Xander. He is becoming a fine young man.

Robin – I will always cherish our friendship. I love you to the moon and back.

Ms. Pentecost – so many years ago but you loved me.

Ashton Fairchild – My tech Guru.

Table of Contents

Chapter 1

"Parents' words become their children's inner voices."

Emily McIntire

As a child, I thought the opposite of fear was terror. However, as an adult, I have realized that although fear is connected to terror, I can heal.

I was born into a family of 13 children, which was common in the 1960s. I have a brother and sister who are younger than me. My mother was considered a genius; I have been told she invented the first waltz dress. She was a Registered Nurse in good standing, but she also struggled with schizophrenia, a condition I did not understand at the time.

I have no memories from before the age of four. After the birth of my little brother, my mother was hospitalized due to a nervous breakdown.

Many people started coming into our house. Some taught classes, while others told of the history, and everything began to breakdown. The treatments she underwent, including electric shock therapy, were confusing to me.

When my mom returned from the hospital, a noticeable change had taken over her. She seemed distant and irritable, almost like a stranger where my loving mother once stood. Seeking solace, she began attending a local Jehovah's Witness church, hoping to find guidance and support. On her very first day back, the pastor delivered a shocking message. He told her that, because of her recent mental breakdown, she was no longer considered one of the 144,000 chosen ones destined for salvation. Instead, he ominously suggested that she had been possessed by Satan himself, urging her to worship him instead. His words left me feeling bewildered and concerned for the woman I once knew so well.

We had so many new friends coming in our house and everything began to revolve around the rituals. I was a mommy's girl and worked hard to impress my mom during these sessions. I did quite well for being only four years old. However, my mom began to lose interest in me and my brother. As a result, I started taking on the caretaker role for my little brother.

While my mom was busy building her coven of thirteen kids, she also began using drugs and drinking. We were even allowed to participate by taking pills. There were white crosses in a bowl on the coffee table, and I learned how much alcohol to add to my brother's bottle.

Drugs, alcohol, rituals, training, and learning all became integral parts of my life. As I reflect on my experiences, alcohol and drugs helped preserve my mental stability; they provided an effective way to dissociate from the challenges I faced.

When I was born, my father had already departed, leaving me to ponder what I might have done wrong. Although I never had the opportunity to meet him, there was a man I came to know as my father the dad of my two youngest siblings. He made it abundantly clear that I was not his child and that he felt no obligation towards me. Growing up, I often felt the weight of that absence, a shadow that loomed over my childhood. I watched as my siblings received the love and attention I longed for, their laughter resonating in a home that felt incomplete. His name appeared on my birth certificate, and I carried his last name.

As I deepened my understanding of our religious practices and embraced the intricacies of my responsibilities, I began to feel a sense of discomfort. However, I recognized the importance of maintaining my mother's love. To achieve this, I felt compelled to excel in my coven's rituals. I internalized all the guidance provided, approached my vows with confidence, and yearned for acceptance within the community.

 # Journaling

My baby, My baby

such a fun baby

lots of giggles lots of love

lots of tummy tickles from the ones I love

Brothers and sisters galore, all of them

changing diapers, feeding and even cleaning my
grubby hands

always having attention, precious in their eyes

they hug me, kiss me and sing a lullaby

I love when I see them, my heart is so full

they know what to do to make me talk and coo

Big large terrazzo floors play would take up a
day

up, up, up, down, down, down

my brother would always catch me

bring the hose in with bubbles

to make a fun play of slip and slide

the Florida room was my favorite place to be

looking out the window to see the great sea

the water would go splash splash

but the boundary was the fence

until I got older and then the beach

where I spent a lot of time

splashing and playing with my toys

When I was urged to wholeheartedly embrace my family's loyalty, to become the most devoted worshiper I could be, and to carry out the responsibilities expected of me, I made a solemn vow to honor these commitments. They also communicated the repercussions of breaking such a vow, instilling in me both a sense of fear and a profound desire to remain true to my promises. At the age of four, nearly five, my life began to transform into ways I had never anticipated.

We lived on a large lake, and my favorite place became the tranquility I experienced while in the water. My house began to transform, with the garage being converted into a new room, and new people started moving in. These changes were unsettling, and I began to feel the growing distance from my family. My siblings and I became estranged, and I found myself yearning for the closeness of our family. My little brother started to grow, and soon he had outgrown all his clothes. I would search through Goodwill boxes, discovering a treasure trove of clothing for myself and my younger siblings. The most remarkable discovery was jackets that fit everyone!

Over time, the peacefulness of my lake underwent significant changes. As our family transitioned from a typical household to one deeply rooted in religious beliefs, new elements were introduced into our environment. One notable addition was the presence of alligator turtles, which my brother brought into the lake. These creatures appeared quite intimidating to me due to their large size and formidable appearance. I was informed that these turtles served a practical purpose: they would consume any remains discarded into the lake, helping to maintain cleanliness and order.

Our property also had a boat that sunk, which became a part of the lake's ecosystem. Remains were sometimes placed within this boat. Despite these changes, the turtles continued to inhabit my lake, and their presence often disturbed my sense of tranquility. I found myself perpetually frightened by their imposing presence, which contrasted sharply with the serenity I once associated with the lake. This transformation reflected not only physical alterations to the environment but also a shift in my emotional experience of the space, blending elements of practicality with underlying fears.

My mother began to change, becoming more serious as she explored new religious pathways. Although she claimed to be happy, her demeanor shifted noticeably.

She stopped showing physical affection, and I felt as though I could do nothing right. As the primary caretaker of my little brother, I devoted much of my attention to him. This was my first attempt to ignore the turmoil surrounding me. I made it a priority to ensure my brother had everything he needed, especially when he would start shaking his arms and legs if I was late with his bottle.

Chaos erupted in my life when I was just five years old. As I started school, I began to show signs of distress, marked by bruises from the indoctrination I experienced. I quickly learned how to respond to questions posed by others, knowing that revealing anything about my home life could lead to severe consequences. The room that had been transformed became a space for rituals where unspeakable events occurred. I found myself trapped in a web of deception.

Reflecting on my past, I find the waves of deception to be quite intriguing. I grapple with the dilemma of remaining loyal to the values instilled by my family or prioritizing my own well-being. Being in school complicated these choices further. When the holidays arrived, I face the decision of either feigning familiarity with the celebrations or admitting that I do not partake in them. Would such honesty raise suspicions among my peers? At just five years old, my instinct was to protect my family, yet the potential consequences for me felt overwhelming.

I was transformed into a troubled child, beginning to rebel and retreat into myself. My family felt nonexistent; my mother had not offered me any warmth or acceptance for months. All I longed for was a simple touch from her. Instead, I encountered my soulmate, whose name I will not reveal, except to say it was reminiscent of a bird. I will always remember the black glove on his left hand. He became the heart of my life, my protector, my friend, and my agent of abuse. He taught me how to love every man and understand their desires.

The new room was transformed into a central hub for our gatherings. My soulmate equipped me for the upcoming day, expressing his deep love for me and the significance of the ritual we were about to undertake. This introduction of terror into my life was profound. While I had learned to navigate fear, the experience of terror was entirely different.

On that fateful day, we convened for a solemn ceremony, standing united before all. I was engulfed in blood, and each person contributed to my indoctrination. This moment marked my acceptance into a new family; I belonged to him, and he belonged to me. Despite the overwhelming pain, I discovered comfort in the fetal position, seeking refuge from the surrounding chaos. That day became a turning point in my life, plunging me into a relentless state of fear. I was only six years old when I was married to him.

I lost my bed and my room, and I was now required to earn my keep for everything I was receiving: a roof over my head, food, a "safe" place, and a new family that would hold me accountable. I began searching for ways to escape, and alcohol and pills provided that relief. We had a doctor assigned to us who became part of our family; he stitched me up after my wedding and alleviated my pain with medication.

I completely lost my sense of self and became a mere bystander in my own life. I yearned for warmth, often feeling cold, yet everything I desired seemed out of reach financially. Gradually, I began to grasp the complexities of the system around me. My soulmate conditioned my body to endure pain, enabling me to serve others and earn my keep. Meanwhile, my mother continued her work as a registered nurse, and I found myself longing for her affection, her love, anything from her. I had to come to terms with the fact that she was unable to provide that now that she had taken on the role of a High Priestess.

I fulfilled my responsibilities, attended school, and lived a facade. At the time, I was unaware that I had become a skilled deceiver to shield my mother. George, our High Priest, also entered our lives. My stepfather was present but remained distant, leaving me puzzled about his role. I recognized that he shielded his children from many hardships.

What I failed to comprehend was that I had taken on a selling role among my family and friends to earn my keep. I lost my life and identity when the men touched me. I was no longer a person... just a product.

I was often in physical pain. Occasionally, my stepfather would come to me during the day, demanding his share. I would plead with him, crying out for him to stop, as I was suffering greatly. Unfortunately, he did not heed my pleas. He owned a gas station, and I can still recall the distinct scent of gasoline, oil, and sweat, along with the memory of his grimy, oily hands reaching out.

I heard a significant amount of construction occurring in the attic, but I was uncertain about the nature of the work. I inquired with others, but they remained tight-lipped. Several weeks later, I finally got a glimpse of the finished space. It turned out to be a completed room featuring two raised bars anchored to the floor. I had hoped it might serve as a bedroom for me, but that was not the case. During this period, I was introduced to the unsettling experience of being groomed.

My little sister and I started spending considerable time in the room, learning how to cater to our customers and fulfill their desires. We had numerous teachers, including our mother, who guided us by maximizing our earnings from the lessons we received. Although I have struggled to discuss the operations of the bars, I can mention that chains and straps were part of the experience. A diverse crowd began to visit, including girls and individuals with dark skin. Some had tattoos covering their bodies, which I found quite intimidating.

At the age of six, I began to gain a better understanding of my body and its functions. I became aware of what was beneficial and what was not. Unfortunately, I started to develop a deep-seated self-hatred, exacerbated by the painful sensations my body emitted, which hindered my ability to perform at my best. I felt inadequate in many aspects of my life, and my soulmate frequently reminded me that I was falling short of their expectations. The repercussions of this realization weighed heavily on me, and I understood that I needed to elevate my efforts, but I was unsure how to do so. I was in a constant state of discomfort, relying on painkillers just to function. My legs often felt like jelly, and I lacked a blanket to keep warm, leaving me perpetually cold. All I longed for was a simple blanket, yet I felt I did not measure up to my family members who could provide me with one.

School was challenging for me; I had become a recluse due to the relentless questions I faced. I struggled to comprehend how those in my life could leave visible scars on me yet expect me to conceal them from others. To protect my family and myself, I became increasingly adept at lying. My misbehavior and quest for attention, particularly from my mother, led to numerous consequences. She often ignored me, and it had been years since I felt her touch. Deep down, I sensed something was amiss within me. I felt as though my own mother despised me. Why? I believed I could be a wonderful daughter if only she would give me a chance. My yearning for love extended beyond my soulmate, yet I found myself uncomfortable with the type of affection he offered.

In a moment of frustration, I made a serious error by expressing my hatred towards a customer and distancing myself from him. He had subjected me to a painful experience, causing me agony. In my distress, I pushed him away and tried to cleanse myself, only to find that the emotional hurt lingered. Overcome with rage, I went downstairs, screaming. It was then that I first encountered the cage. I saw others bringing in a dog cage and placing it in the hallway leading to the laundry room. They confined me within it, punishing me for disrespecting one of their valued clients. I should have managed my anger and hidden the pain I felt. I remained in the cage for what seemed like an eternity, even days.

As I sat for hours in my cage, I remained lost in my thoughts, trying to make sense of my situation. How did I end up here? Why couldn't I grasp what was happening around me? I felt a strange sense of confidence, believing I was doing the right things and accepting the consequences of my mistakes, even as I developed a very distorted way of thinking. I had somehow become the embodiment of my disobedience that led me to this place. Yet, I was at a loss for how to change it. I realized I had invested my entire life in the pursuit of recognition and love. Now, I found myself confined, with no food or water, and nowhere to relieve myself except in the corner. My family, including my mom and George, along with my siblings, would often walk past my cage and kick it, making me stumble and reinforce the foolishness I felt. The humiliation was overwhelming. I could not shake the thought that I was in this situation because someone had caused me pain. My longing to belong to this family diminished, yet I saw no alternative but to keep striving for their acceptance.

During one of the many times I found myself confined to my cage, I began to ponder a profound thought. I wanted to believe that this reflection helped save me, fueled my determination, and offered me a glimpse of hope for my future. As I observed my siblings, I realized I was the only child among thirteen with blue eyes. This unique trait instilled a sense of power within me, even if it remained concealed on the outside. My father also had blue eyes, perhaps a sign of my difference. Maybe I did not truly belong to this family. After all, my eyes were blue! This realization energized me, reinforcing my resolve to resist becoming like them. I recognized my uniqueness, but the question remained: how could I escape? I understood that I was trapped until I could find a way out.

"The process of dissociation is an elegant mechanism built into the human psychological system as a form of escape from (sometimes literally) going crazy. The problem with checking out so thoroughly is that it can leave us feeling dead inside, with little or no ability to feel our feelings in our bodies."

Alexandra Katehakis

My inner child's passion for self-expression through writing inspires me to fully engage in this journey. As I navigate this unfamiliar path, I realize that I am growing and learning alongside her. Allow me to introduce Charlotte, a bright and inquisitive girl aged 4 to 6, who initially feels considerable confusion as we embark on this new chapter in our lives. I also have a little sister named Victoria, who is 4 years old. She and I share a close bond, and she is such a sweet child. I often helped her when she cried or felt hungry because I loved her and cherished her sweetness. She showered me with kisses and enjoyed sleeping beside me. Victoria used to follow me around a lot. When I was four and she was two, our world turned upside down, and we became a family or a coven, as I like to say.

After the attic was completed, I spent a considerable amount of time there alone, but eventually, my little sister began to join me. It felt comforting to have her company. However, they also sent men up there for her, and that drove me to the brink of madness. Watching her suffering, screaming at the top of her lungs, left me feeling utterly helpless, as I was bound by my own rules and consequences. I often lost my grip on reality, and as I reflect on that time, I find myself questioning whether I was deceived or if I truly witnessed what transpired. My mother always left me feeling confused, and I sometimes wonder if events unfolded as I remember or if she was playing a game with me.

Charlotte needed me to document this. One morning, while we were in the attic with the apparatus, my baby sister appeared unwell; in fact, she seemed almost lifeless, though she moved slightly. The big man continued to do cruel things to her, and on a few occasions, I had to cover my eyes and think of something else. When I finally managed to focus on my baby sister again, she was beneath the apparatus so still, bleeding from her private area, and looking like a discarded piece of trash. She didn't move at all. After completing my task, I went downstairs and curled up in a fetal position, losing track of how many days passed.

For several days, I didn't see my baby sister. I lost control and soiled myself because I couldn't unwrap my legs from my body. When it was time for me to return to the attic, I found my little sister there. She resembled my sister but felt different. I couldn't discern whether I truly remembered my little sister, perhaps believing she had recovered, or if she had actually passed and this was someone else entirely. This confusion occurred frequently, and as an adult, I still struggle to process the truth. I had to call her Queen Victoria, but she was unkind. The affection she once showed me had transformed into cruel words, mocking me for not having a father, and she seemed like a different sister altogether. Was this truly my little sister, or was she someone else? She turned against me, and I became her victim, too.

Around this time, a teacher, Ms. Pentecost, took an interest in me. She greeted me each morning at school and frequently checked on me throughout the day. Occasionally, she would offer me something delicious to eat at lunch. I began to warm up to her and looked forward to the smile she would give me upon seeing me. She asked me all kinds of questions in various ways, yet I remained loyal to my family, blaming myself for the marks on my body and my peculiar habits in the restroom, another story altogether. I felt a sense of pride in navigating this acceptance while maintaining my family's loyalty.

She had a way of encouraging me to hold on to hope during times I felt defeated. At Christmas time in her class, I once again explained to her that our family did not celebrate the holiday. I became invisible during this time, longing to be a part of it but knowing the consequences. After the party, she called me up to her desk and handed me a present. She asked me to open it in front of her, and we would keep it hidden in her class so I could see it each day. It was a book of lifesavers, so neatly arranged that it resembled a treasure. I cherished that little secret, and she assured me I did not have to tell anyone. I loved going to her class, but within a couple of months, she was gone, and we did not return to school. It was summertime, and I knew what that meant for my life.

I was now seven years old, and fear dominated my existence. There is nowhere I could find solace. With school out for the summer, I left my lifesavers behind in the classroom, too terrified to take them with me. While others celebrate the end of the school year, I was overwhelmed by the implications this had for me. I would be home all day, with more time to earn money, while they could do whatever they wish to me without facing any consequences. The bruises on my face had worsened, the cuts had deepened, and my clientele had expanded.

I traveled a few cities away to a large homeless beach area. We rented an apartment with exterior stairs and a white building. Not all my siblings came; many chose to stay at our home. My mom and George stayed across the street while I was remaining in the white apartment. The inside of the apartment was frightening, with a single light hanging down, a metal table, and cobwebs everywhere. I was too scared to sleep there without a lock on the door. I began sleeping on a beach, which was common in that area. On my very first day there, I understood why I was in this situation. The dog racing track was just a block away. The new men were different in ways I cannot articulate. Most had money but craved more excitement. I performed but became numb in the process. I despised myself; I loathed my life, feeling unlovable because I was a bad kid that no one was pleased with. I began to act out a little more, not much, but I continued to cling to the hope of being different.

An apparatus was brought into the apartment that allowed both men and women to use straps around my wrists, along with various types of whips. There were also different devices they could apply to my body, some equipped with spikes. The lovemaking experience was unlike anything I had known, and I often found myself zoning out during these moments. To escape the reality of my situation, I began taking pills to numb my feelings and dull my awareness of what was happening. It always concluded in the same manner – pay the lady across the street. This period of my life was incredibly frightening; I often questioned whether I would survive. I continued to bleed profusely, especially as they employed different instruments on me.

 # Journaling

Man after man

Legs fall asleep

Move legs

Sick I'm sick

Stomach ache

Dog races

Room

Men

I just lay there

they did all the stuff

One happy memory I hold on to is from the 4th of July. I believe someone mentioned it to me, but I recall standing in the middle of the neighborhood street with a bent straight hanger and a Brillo pad. I attached the Brillo pad to the end of the hanger and spun it around, striking the street. Sparks flew from the Brillo as it made contact, and for a moment, it brought a smile to my face.

Chapter 2

I endured the most terrifying summer of my life before others came. My little person, Charlotte, wants to share her thoughts and feelings. *Mommy, I promise to be good. I will take care of you if you want me to. I can, Mommy, but they are hurting me, and they said it is okay with you. Mommy, am I your baby anymore? Can I have a blanket, Mommy? Why am I trapped in this cage? My heart is turning black, I just need you to touch me, mommy. Am I doing okay, Mommy? Mommy, may I sleep with you? Do you know they make me bleed, do you know what they do to me? Mommy, please help me. No? Do you not care about me? I can be good, Mommy, if you would just tell me. I did not understand. I may be just a baby, but I promise not to bother you or ask for anything. Mommy, I want you to love me again. Please, I will do better; I will not scream, and I will be your big girl. Mommy, what did I do wrong?*

I spent most nights on the beach, retreating to the apartment during the day. With numerous visitors coming to see me, I lost track of the numbers. As people came and went, I often contemplated returning to the beach later, knowing I could rejuvenate myself in the evenings. Occasionally, I would sleep on the pier, but it never felt safe; I felt trapped with no escape, making the beach a much safer option with more avenues for retreatment. I found immense peace on the beach, liberated from the need to perform for anyone. This area was where my soulmate originated, and he had friends. He took me to the Diamond Bar, where he introduced me to many new acquaintances. I vividly remember wearing fishnet tights and dancing on the tables, feeling both scared and exhilarated by the attention as hands reached out to touch me. The affection left me utterly confused.

One day, my mom came to the apartment, startling me by banging open the door. She appeared wild-eyed and frantic, speaking in a disjointed manner. Her erratic behavior had been increasing, but this time she felt different. Before I could react, she shoved me to the ground and began striking my head against the hard floor. I screamed for help, but no one was around. She restrained me with straps, leaving me barely able to move. As she violated my boundaries, she claimed my soulmate had informed her of my actions in the bar. I promise I was unaware of any wrongdoing; the way I danced, without panties, and the attention from men were not approved by my mother. She inflicted pain to teach me a lesson. Afterward, I lay on the floor, bleeding from my head and injuries. The doctor arrived later to stitch up my wounds.

I was eager to return home and go back to school. Eventually, we did, and the remainder of the summer was quite peaceful. I experienced healing both emotionally and physically, and my head began to feel better. My hair was also starting to grow back, but I was aware that if it did not grow quickly enough, I would have to cut it short again. This gradual regrowth allowed it to blend in, which spared me from having to explain anything.

In our home, we had beautiful terrazzo floors. I fondly recall the times when I would bring the hose into the living room, turning it on and pouring dish soap onto the floors. My siblings and I would gleefully slip and slide all over the house, creating joyful memories. Although these moments were rare, I wished they would last forever. We always managed to clean up before the adults returned, keeping it as our little secret.

School began, and I entered third grade filled with excitement about being away from home and reuniting with my teacher. The first thing I wanted to do was see the "treasure" she had kept for me. However, upon arriving at my classroom, I was disheartened to find it was not the same room, and my teacher was absent. In a panic, I rushed down the hall in search of my class, only to encounter a different teacher instead. Overwhelmed with emotion, I left school in tears, feeling lost and uncertain about how to find my teacher. I returned the next day, hoping to see her, but she was nowhere to be found. I felt as though I had lost my treasure. This year brought significant changes within me. I found myself sitting at the back of the class, indifferent to my appearance, neglecting personal hygiene, and wishing to go unnoticed. I became increasingly isolated, grappling with feelings of despair and wishing I could simply disappear.

Journaling

Ms. Pentecost use to touch my face and was very soft. She would give me food. I would go the long way sometimes just to see her. When my hair was a "rats nest" she would brush it and tell me how shiny it was. Ms. Pentecost brought me some shorts they were a pretty pink. One day she told me about the period and asked me if it happened and I said no and she said I had blood on my shorts. I told her it was a bad night and she took me to the teachers place and wiped blood off of me and dried me and hugged me and gave me more shorts to wear. Whenever she saw me she would get a big smile from me, like she liked me. I loved Ms. Pentecost

I often find myself feeling angry when others hurt me. I started to realize that the other kids at school did not discuss the same things I did, which made me hold back my feelings, as I was an incredibly angry little girl. The cage became a familiar place for me, as I spent a lot of time there. If only I had a blanket; it was my favorite and most comforting item, allowing me to feel invisible and safe.

Journaling

Ms. Pentecost.   Thank you for all you did for me in my short time knowing you.   Today I am doing work on the things I could never tell you about. When I was so sad but acting ok my mom was in a cult and I was really being hurt.   Remember when I had blood on my bottom and you cleaned me up, I was having to perform for different men and they hurt me in my bottom area.   Thank you for loving me when I had you.   That may have been the last time I felt love.   Closed down a lot after you disappeared.   On weekends I would stay under the Elephant Ears and wait for Monday. All the times you asked me what was happening I couldn't tell you.   I have a therapist now that I told those things to.   I was scared to tell you because I wasn't allowed.   I'm doing it now.   Remember the time I had the lines on my shirt and you asked me why and I told you a cat scratched me down my back.   I lied to you.   I escaped my cage and my mom made me get on my hands and knees with my head in the cage and used an electric cord on my back.   I'm so sorry for the many lies I told you.   When you gave me good tight hugs I felt so safe.   Thank you for loving me.   I'm using you to help me love inner child now.   Thank you for showing me.

Things began to change significantly at home as well. I became adept at discerning who was nearby simply by listening to footsteps. I could recognize my mom's footsteps by heart and knew when she was approaching. I could even differentiate which version of my mom was coming based on the sound of her steps. If her footsteps were loud and angry, I would pretend to be asleep. Conversely, if they were soft and gentle, I initially believed it signaled her intention to comfort me. However, I soon realized that those were often the moments when she was being sneaky, trying to scare me. She managed to catch me off guard a couple of times, but my hearing became so finely tuned that I could detect even the faintest sounds and identify their source. I was aware of my soulmates and often concealed my true self in anticipation of his arrival, yet I could never fully prepare for him. Each encounter left me puzzled, as it always felt distinct and unique.

As my anger intensified with each passing day, I came to understand that harboring such feelings was unkind to me. Erupting in anger led to numerous consequences, often leaving me feeling as though I were on the brink of collapse. The repercussions stemmed from various individuals, and it was particularly humiliating when my siblings began to confine me in a cage. I found myself crying frequently, which provided a sense of safety. Over time, I came to understand in therapy that crying and sobbing had become my "safe" emotions. While expressing anger led to consequences, sobbing allowed me to remain unreactive. I could cry without anyone disturbing me, and this act became my refuge. Crying transformed into my "pet" emotion, a source of comfort I turned to regularly.

Journaling

My rage is sacred because it is mine. I cannot take it away from Charlotte. She has every right to be rageful and if I take it she will lose her identity. Oh Charlotte, how do I nurture you? How do I do this with so much balled within me. You deserve so much better than I can give you right now. Trying to get validation from within is so hard. 3 weeks. Where do I get everything out? I feel so lost and alone. I need to get some energy back. But it has to come from within and I feel so depleted. Does support not come from outside too? I get so confused. Charlotte is begging for supportive people in her life. Why not me?

I felt lost and isolated, facing a world that seemed to turn against me. As men started to re-enter my life, I found joy in the opportunity to leave my room, the cage. Gradually, I began to mature and gain a clearer understanding of my circumstances, though my thoughts and emotions remained tangled and perplexing.

The ritual room became increasingly crowded, and I never missed a meeting. I witnessed many things that a child should not see. But was I truly a child? I felt like one, as I cried constantly, earning myself a variety of shameful nicknames from my people. Yet, beneath the surface of my anger, I was gaining experience at a remarkably early age, able to meet the expectations of everyone I encountered. Was I a baby or an adult? This confusion about my identity began to deepen.

Rituals were conducted, reinforcing the vows I had taken. I was required to participate fully, as there was no way to excuse myself from my commitments. Within the ritual room, my vows felt more significant than they did outside. My soulmate appeared strict with others, emphasizing our betrothal, and seeming to protect me. However, outside the room, he allowed anyone to treat me as they wished. I was uncertain whether my betrothal to him was permanent or limited to the confines of the ritual space. The meaning of being married to him remained unclear to me.

I lived in a fantasy, which I now understand served as a protector. I learned to ignore the distress of my brothers and sisters during rituals. I managed to block out their screams, sounds, and pleas. Although I wanted to comfort them, I knew that was forbidden, so I devised a way to cope. My mind began to vibrate, and my ears would ring to shield me from the cries. I was determined to preserve my compassion, so my body found a way to manage the noise. I often dreamed of a different reality, one where I had loving parents. The vibrations in my head and the ringing in my ears facilitated this escape.

Chapter 3

> *"To lose a child, to have her spirited away like something from a fairy tale, surely that must be every mother's nightmare."*
>
> *Elly Griffiths*

During this time, I encountered a breeding experience. My older sister chose to become a baby breeder for an upcoming ritual. I understood this meant she would be impregnated in April to deliver at six months, making the birth less noticeable. Halloween, also known as Samhain, was the designated time for the delivery. This was explained to us in a teaching session, which frightened and upset me when my sister raised her hand to participate. The significance of the ritual was described in detail, and as I listened, my heart sank. I tried to dissuade my sister, but she believed this would earn her immense acceptance from Satan. We were all seeking acceptance in our own ways. My sister had to stop taking the pill prescribed by Dr. G. Eventually, she confided in me that she was pregnant, though she was unsure how it happened. I was equally confused, but I noticed her stomach began to swell. The day of reckoning arrived.

My mother had acquired a piece of land approximately 75 miles from our home. The area was swampy, filled with alligators and snakes. The journey felt endless, but when we finally arrived, I saw an Airstream recreational vehicle on the property. I grew to despise this RV and the land it occupied. I had been informed that it was located near a paper mill, and as we approached, the stench from the mill was unmistakable. It made my nose sting; the odor was so sharp and overwhelming.

During our brief stay in this RV, I found myself sleeping on the floor, which was covered in orange shag carpet. The odor emanating from the carpet was unlike anything I had ever encountered before. It was quite difficult to rest on it, particularly without any blankets to mask the smell. The RV was situated by a small creek inhabited by fish with elongated snouts, which appeared as if they could pierce through skin, much like a needle. My brother would take instruction from our High Priest to throw the younger ones in. I panicked when the fish came near me and almost drowned trying to scream and swim, fearing the fish would get me. It felt like fear was all over the place, there was no place that was safe.

Two days later, on the day of Samhain, everyone was up early. My sister wore a special garment. Her face bore an expression I had never seen before; she did not look like my sister, even though I knew she was. Her robe was a shiny red adorned with white and black markings, and she wore a crown on her head. She looked beautiful. I noticed her teeth were white, a stark contrast to mine, as we never had the brushes we needed to clean our teeth. Kids used to say I had green teeth, which was deeply shaming for me. Seeing her white teeth stood out vividly in my mind.

We were forbidden to approach or touch my sister, as she had been specially anointed. Although I had no understanding of what that entailed, she was off-limits that day. We participated in numerous ceremonies, honoring the religion of Satanism and offering our praise and adoration. I distinctly recalled an animal sacrifice I made, particularly a turtle I discovered. He was of average size, and during one ceremony, I was tasked with killing him using a knife. Unable to crack his shell, my brother stepped in and delivered a powerful blow, causing a splatter. I was surprised to learn that turtles had blood, and a mark of that blood was placed on my forehead. I felt indifferent towards this death, as it had become increasingly common for me to witness.

As dusk fell, a somber atmosphere enveloped everyone. My brothers built a fire that blazed larger than the one that had flickered throughout the afternoon. My sister vanished from view, and I lost track of her whereabouts. Overwhelmed by a sense of impending doom, I began to cry uncontrollably, drawing reprimands for my distress. Deep down, I sensed that a significant loss was imminent, though I could not tell if it was a premonition or something I had heard discussed back in April.

I recall feeling an overwhelming sense of anxiety that evening, leading me to take more pills than I should have. In hindsight, I am grateful for my actions as I began to understand the gravity of the situation unfolding before me. Her soulmate started to massage her stomach, then removed all her clothing. The pressure of the rubbing intensified in her abdominal area. She began to sob, scream, and panic, fighting against everyone around her, pleading for them to stop. Yet, they persisted. I remember noticing blood around her eyes, though it might have been a side effect of the pills I had taken. Suddenly, a tremendous, piercing scream erupted, and a baby emerged, crying.

My eyes widened in shock, as I was bewildered by the arrival of this newborn. My sister's scream was not one of pain, but rather a chilling, deadly cry.

My mother and our High Priest brought a tiny baby close to my sister's face so she could see him. As she reached out to touch him, they pulled the baby away, revealing gnashing teeth. A heart-wrenching scream escaped her lips as her baby vanished from view. They returned the baby near her, and her soulmate began to cut away parts of him. Both the baby and my sister were in agony, their cries intertwining in a haunting melody that lingers in my memory. The baby's screams were softer, likely due to his underdeveloped state. He appeared different from the babies I have encountered less developed yet still viable. I cannot recall what transpired afterward, only that there were reasons for choosing a location surrounded by alligators.

My sister gradually regained her physical strength, and her soulmate, filled with pride, cared for her with great tenderness. This support reassured her that she had made the right choice. She grew significantly stronger in her role during the ceremonies. While the memory of the baby began to fade, I could never shake the haunting images I had witnessed.

We extended our stay at the RV for a few more days, primarily to allow my sister to heal. She wore a crown on her head and behaved as if nothing had happened. I struggled to understand how she could carry on while my heart grew heavy and dark, after witnessing what my family had done. I felt trapped, unable to escape, as I was only nine years old. The following day, while running around the property, I accidentally stepped on a pronged fish lure. The five-point prong pierced through my big toe and emerged next to my toenail, causing excruciating pain. At that time, my mother was a nurse, and our doctor was present in case there were complications with the baby. However, they did not alleviate my pain or remove the lure. They didn't even clip off a piece of the prong to help slide it out. Instead, I had to hide under the kitchen table in the RV for the remainder of the day. Each movement caused the lure to snag in the orange shag carpet, intensifying my agony. That night, I slept under the table with the lure still embedded in my toe, barely managing to rest due to the pain. The next day, we returned home, and I went to the hospital. To my relief, they clipped a prong and easily slid it out. Upon returning home, I was confined to a cage because my mom believed I was trying to draw attention to myself when the focus should have been entirely on my sister.

I deeply regretted taking that attention away from her and vowed never to seek the spotlight again.

The next couple years were pretty "normal" continuing to cultivate our understanding of the ceremonies and becoming better at honoring Satan through our practices.

We frequently visited our property, which allowed me to spend more time on myself and reflect on the memories I had tucked away in my heart. My brothers and their friends were busy constructing various projects on the land, preparing it for whatever lay ahead. During this time, we built numerous fires, honing our technique for lighting them based on the wind's direction and the pungent odor from the nearby paper mill. Our aim was to blend the two scents, creating a unique aroma. Although it was a challenging endeavor, I felt we had mastered it, as the smell was so overpowering that it was nearly unbearable to be outside.

Life continued, and the acts of service persisted. One day, my mom and our High Priest summoned us to the learning room. We dedicated the day to exploring the history of human sacrifices, understanding the distinctions between breeding and sacrifices, and examining the implications of these acts. I found it difficult to focus during the instruction, leaving me uncertain about my understanding of the material being taught. Regardless, I was unprepared for what transpired next.

Chapter 4

> *"In situations of captivity the perpetrator becomes the most powerful person in the life of the victim, and the psychology of the victim is shaped by the actions and beliefs of the perpetrator."*
>
> Judith Lewis Herman

We had a station wagon with bench seats in the back. The adults announced that we would be embarking on a new experience now that we were older. I was between 10 and 11 years old. The only ones I remember in the station wagon were my younger brother and sister, an older brother, my mom, and an assistant to the High Priest. As we began driving, my little sister, brother, and I settled into the bench seats in the back. During the drive, as we chatted among ourselves, we noticed that we were taking a different route. My younger sister, who was quite perceptive, began discussing the new instructions they had talked about the other day. She mentioned human sacrifices, homeless people, and taking them to the property. I was taken aback; I hadn't heard any of this before. How could I have been so distracted to miss all this? She started explaining the procedure, and suddenly, my head began to vibrate, and my ears rang. I remember saying, "I'm scared." I began to shake and pay close attention again. It had been foolish of me to be talking, playing, and joking in the back of the station wagon. I should have been more observant.

We were heading downtown to a questionable area. I was keenly observing every move being made, and I didn't like what I was hearing. The ones in the front of the station wagon were discussing the best place to avoid being noticed. The car slowed several times before finally coming to a stop. I looked around; it was pitch black, and I couldn't see anything. The street was very worn, littered with debris visible in the headlights. My brother and the assistant jumped out of the car, grabbed a man, and as my mom was sliding down the window, they threw this smelly, underdressed man with oily hair into the back of the station wagon with us. They quickly jumped back into the car, and my mother sped off. What just happened? I was confused and attempted to engage with the man who was inquiring about what was happening. My sister cautioned me against communicating with him, reminding me that I was not supposed to. I realized I hadn't been paying attention that day, and now I regret it. I was unaware of the situation, and I disliked that feeling. I looked directly into the man's eyes, trying to convey my lack of understanding. We made a turn, and I noticed we were now headed to the property. But for what purpose? I wished I had listened more carefully. I felt foolish for allowing this to continue without a clear understanding of the instructions.

I made eye contact with the man whenever I could, hoping to convey through my gaze that I was not involved in the situation. I wish he noticed my blue eyes. Eventually, we reached our property, and the first thing that struck me was the Airstream. I despised this place, filled with memories I longed to erase. As we arrived, everyone emerged, likely having been there for some time. I surveyed the property and observed the new projects that had been completed, though the unpleasant smell lingered just as strongly. My little sister pointed out another detail I had overlooked in the instructions. My mother had bought this place because of the odor from the paper mill; she claimed it masked the scent of burning flesh. WHAT?! She explained that the smell from the paper mill, much like that of sewage treatment plants, could obscure the stench of human remains. My head began to throb, and my ears rang, prompting me to sit down. Then, I spotted a cross like the one at home, positioned near the water, as my sister mentioned. The vibrations intensified, and I felt as though I might faint. As afternoon faded into evening, a solemn ceremony unfolded. No child should ever have to witness the haunting images and endure the acrid stench that lingered in the air that night. I found myself lost in my thoughts, attempting to shield myself from the reality around me, while the anguished cries and moans of a homeless man echoed in my ears. Overwhelmed by guilt and shame, I couldn't bring myself to look at him. I wished I could convey my sorrow and discontent with the ceremony. Should I confide in someone? Did I even want to continue living? How would my family react if I spoke out? What about my neighbors who lived next door to us? Who could I trust with my fears? Who would listen to a child like me? Ultimately, fear of my family silenced me, and I chose to remain quiet. The next thing I knew, I was awakening to a completed scene. The sun was rising, and most people were still asleep. I sat there, studying the figure before me, reflecting on the events of the previous night. His skeleton lay intact, yet devoid of a face. His arms and legs appeared twisted together, as if bound in a grotesque embrace. A child should never have to bear witness to such horrors. Yet, I did.

Life continued, and this became a familiar occurrence. Yet, I will never forget the first man, the first images, the first awakening, and the first scent that lingered in my memory. Although these experiences became routine, I never felt comfortable in that station wagon with its bench seats again. I attempted to convey my differences to each of them through my eyes and body language, but I was never able to save a single one. The ceremonies became commonplace, and I began to feel indifferent to the entire process. I surrendered my emotions, sitting there, unable to engage any of my senses. I could no longer see, smell, or hear anything, and my sense of touch and taste had vanished early in my life. It was strange to be a child who could turn their senses on and off at will; it became a peculiar, yet useful, tool.

In the place where I grew up, we didn't experience distinct seasons, but there were subtle shifts in temperature. During winter, it felt cold to me. I often found myself without warm clothes or a blanket, and memories of the Goodwill Boxes from my childhood came flooding back. I revisited that resource, now more for my own needs than for my siblings. While I was away from home, I wore a coat, but I kept it hidden in a bag beneath my favorite Elephant Ears plant; that was my secret hiding spot. I also came to realize that those boxes provided safe spaces to sleep warm and comforting.

Chapter 5

> *"In order to get past something terrible, sometimes you have to walk through the pain, not around it. It might be messy. It might make you sob. But if you let yourself cry long enough, you finally reach the bottom of your tears."*
> *Michelle Knight*

Something was brewing; I had developed a keen discernment of most people, allowing me to sense that an important event was on the horizon. It felt as though I was privy to a significant secret, and that secret was me. I felt as though I could read people's intentions and had an extrasensory perception because most events I contemplated eventually came to pass. I find it difficult to describe this phenomenon in any other way. We all gathered in the Ritual Room one evening, sitting in a circle. I found myself brought to the center, where I was faced with a question that filled me with dread, as I was suddenly the center of attention. George and my mother led the meeting. My mother informed me that I had been chosen to breed a child this year. We were always given the option to choose a consequence in place of the offer. She explained that if I decided against fulfilling this obligation, the consequence would be that I would be 'fixed,' rendering me unable to have children in the future. I was given two hours to contemplate my decision. For a 12-year-old, this was a significant decision. I asked, "Mommy, can I talk to you? I don't understand." She became fiercely agitated, running around the room, while George dismissed us, saying we would return in two hours.

I stepped outside, lingering near Elephant Ears, a plant I grew to love. I had grown too large to sit beneath them, yet I still found comfort in their presence. Memories of my sister flooded my mind, recalling the challenges she faced two years ago. I could never harm a baby, especially one that came from me. But what does that mean for others? Would there be no babies at all? How could that even happen? I was faced with a difficult decision, and once again, I found myself without anyone to confide in, to guide me, or to clarify the implications of my choices. It was just me. When will I finally understand? I hope it will be soon. It feels like there is no one here for me, and I need to accept that. Even today, I find myself waiting for the right person to appear, though I know deep down that it may never happen. I long for someone to help me make decisions, to confide in when I'm hurting, and to simply sit with me, offering comfort in her embrace. Yet, I harbor so much resentment toward my mother, and I struggle to comprehend why I still crave this connection. I don't want these feelings to come from her, yet paradoxically, I do. It confuses me even today.

As I stepped back into the room, I found everyone gathered there, including my mother. She appeared calm and completely at ease, her eyes slightly glazed. I returned to the center stage, feeling an overwhelming sense of discomfort. My emotions were in turmoil, and I began to question the members of this coven. When would it be my turn to make my own choices? You have presented me with a lose-lose situation. How can you expect me to have a baby? If I choose to keep it, will I be allowed to? Why are you putting me through this? You all know how much I cared for my brother and sister. I love children; how can this be fair? I glanced around the room, but no one seemed to respond. Some stared blankly at me, while others yawned, lost in their own thoughts. Was this not significant to them? I couldn't decipher my older sister's expression; there was no hint of how she felt about the situation.

I struggled to comprehend the idea of having a baby only to have it cut up like my sisters. It was unfathomable to me that anyone would think I would even consider such a thing. I couldn't grasp the other perspective, how could they possibly 'fix' me? Would that mean no babies ever? How did they even manage to do this? I simply couldn't bear the thought of having a child for my mother. How much more hatred could she direct at me? After much contemplation, I made my decision. I resolved to accept the consequences, and with that announcement, I ran out of the room in tears. Sitting there, I realized that I didn't know how long I would be alive, so why not face the punishment instead of a baby facing it. That was my thought process. I didn't want to live much longer. I felt ok with my decision, at least a baby would not be hurt. I could deal with whatever happens to me.

The following day, we reconvened in the Ritual Room. This time, I found myself on the table, exposed to everyone. Lying on my back, a rod was inserted into my private parts. Initially, this was tolerable, but soon I began to feel an intense heat radiating from the rod. My insides felt as if they were igniting, and I lost consciousness shortly thereafter. When I regained awareness, I discovered I was in my cage, experiencing significant pain. Our doctor arrived to assess my condition and administer some medication

As I return to writing, I want my readers to know that I took a break. My inner child needed to feel comfortable with what I was sharing. After much reflection, discussions with my therapist Noel, and nurturing that child, I am now back and have received my child's permission to continue my writing journey.

Eventually, I found a way to recover. I experienced immense grief over my decision, as my love for children was profound. I often questioned my choices and wondered about the value of life itself. During that difficult period, I contemplated suicide numerous times. The pain I felt was nearly unbearable, and the smirks from my family as they passed by my confinement were incredibly hard to endure. I was uncertain whether to feel relieved about not having a baby, yet the thought of it was unbearable. Later, I discovered that they had inseminated me while I was unconscious, right at the moment when the consequences were unfolding. I found out I was pregnant, and I felt deceived. The pain was overwhelming, and I realized that one of the men had violated me. At the time, I didn't understand the implications of that, and my mind struggled to comprehend everything that was happening. I couldn't articulate the emotions I was experiencing as I looked toward the future. I was filled with dread and did not want to face this reality.

They claimed I was their choice, and even though I faced the consequences, I still had to contribute to my family's needs. My inner girl continues to experience the heartbreak and pain she has endured. A baby? I longed for happiness, but I knew what would unfold in six months. Should I embrace it or pretend it didn't exist? What was a 12-year-old person supposed to do? I desperately wanted someone to confide in, someone with whom I could share my foolish decision and how I had been deceived. Please, someone listen to me. Please, someone, love me. Please.

During this time, DCFS visited our home after someone filed a report against us. They informed my mother about their scheduled inspection. My hope was high! My mother instructed us on how to behave and what not to say; she and my stepfather would handle the conversation.

On the day of the interview, I was filled with the hope of being taken away from my family. I sat on my stepfather's lap, and we presented ourselves as a picture-perfect set of children. Yet, deep down, I longed for them to see the truth. I wished my eyes would reveal everything. However, they left, stating they saw nothing was wrong. That day, I shed genuine tears of sadness. Please, take me away.

As my belly began to grow, I found myself grappling with a whirlwind of emotions. Was I filled with excitement or overshadowed by sadness as I contemplated the impending outcome? My mind started to conjure up various scenarios: perhaps I could snatch the baby away the moment it arrived, unnoticed by others. Or maybe I could escape the night before, seeking a life solely for myself and my baby. In darker moments, I even entertained the thought of resorting to violence, imagining a world where only my baby and I would remain. `

The day arrived, transitioning from daylight to darkness. I was still uncertain about how to save the baby. I had acquired a crown, similar to the one my sister wore, which granted me a sense of vulnerability. It was a crucial rule during the ritual: observe, but do not touch. My soulmate began to rub my belly vigorously, and I was overwhelmed with sobs and screams, contemplating my next move to rescue the baby. As my soulmate pressed into my stomach, I felt a sharp pop, and the pain intensified horrifically. I screamed in agony and caught sight of my mother near the place where the baby was emerging. Anger surged within me at the unfolding events. In a fit of rage, I pulled my knee up and struck my mother in the face, fueled by my fury. Blood began to flow from her injury. Desperate to reach my baby, I realized it was a girl, but George intervened, taking the baby and declaring her name to be Miranda. I loathed that name; it felt like something a witch would bear. While the doctor attended to my mother, I was left bleeding and alone.

I attempted to see my baby, but I was bleeding profusely and felt so weak that I couldn't rise to look for her. Finally, the doctor arrived to tend to me, and the bleeding ceased. Anger surged within me, so intensely that it felt as if blood were streaming from my eyes. Then, I caught sight of her. That was my baby, and I felt utterly powerless to help her. I began to sob uncontrollably as I heard her distant cries. Then, silence enveloped the area. She was gone. I will never forget her appearance, and in my mind, I named her Rebecca. I either did not see or perhaps have blocked out the painful reality of her sacrificial loss.

Journaling

God has to be me. My heart is black.
How can I love me. Do I just go up and
hug the baby and say I love you and
that will make it all better?

Chapter 6

Life changed dramatically for me after that loss. I found myself consumed by anger, struggling to express it in a healthy way. My empathy for others diminished, and I felt a profound shift within myself after an altercation with my mother. I began to feel almost invincible, ready to confront anyone who crossed my path. This newfound aggression led to frequent fights at school, which caused the principal to treat me differently than he had before. I faced detentions and suspensions for the conflicts that seemed beyond my control. In a misguided attempt at self-protection, I always carried a knife with me at that time.

I felt as though they had triumphed, and I had become one of them. I found myself just as consumed by anger and violence as they were. Despite my childhood aspiration to be different, I noticed that as I grew older, I began to mirror their behaviors. The sense of compassion and care I once had for others faded away.

I had transformed into a hardened individual, resorting to cursing more often than engaging in meaningful conversation. My alcohol consumption escalated, and pills, acid and Quaaludes became my sole source of optimism. I ensnared as many young people in the grip of addiction as I could, watching with a twisted sense of satisfaction as their families mothers and fathers crumbled around them, all while I provided the pills that fueled their decline. At that point, I had lost all sense of care for anything.

Right before I turned 13, my mother had another breakdown and became "reincarnated" into a dog. I was so sick of her and hated her with everything in me. She had become an embarrassment to me. I had none of those feelings of wanting her acceptance anymore, although deep down that caused a lot of my anger.

One day during that period, my mother approached me at the bus stop on all fours, resembling a dog. While I could manage such behavior at home, her appearance at the bus stop was unacceptable. I felt humiliated in front of the kids I desperately wanted to impress. They laughed at me, pointing fingers and declaring that my family was strange, implying that I was just like them. As I walked home, tears streamed down my face, not from sadness, but from anger I could hear the taunts of the kids behind me, with my mother trailing behind on all fours once more.

Soon thereafter, I fell into a deep depression and withdrew from communication. My words felt meaningless, leading me to stop trying to engage with others. I was a chaotic version of myself, far from who I aspired to be. My behavior mirrored that of my family, and I found myself getting into physical altercations with my siblings, fueled by my inner fury. The most profound disappointment in this transformation was the realization that I had always hoped my father would come to my rescue from my mother. With this newfound streak of violence, I understood that he would never return. That dream was shattered; he had never been fond of angry individuals, which I assumed was the reason he left my mother and now, me.

As I strolled around my lake one day, a boy who rode the bus and happened to be there that day called me over. I continued walking, choosing to ignore him, as I suspected he wanted to tell me how strange I was. From that day forward, I embraced the labels 'Weird' and 'Freak' as new definitions of myself. There was a yard with a fence that extended into the water, requiring a swim to get past it. Upon reaching the other side of the property, I was making my way down the fence line towards shallow water when the boy appeared. I later learned his name was David. He began sharing with me that his mother had polio and could not walk without crutches. He expressed his frustration about how the other kids made fun of her, and how much he despised it. As I continued walking, he trailed behind, engaging me in conversation. He expressed deep concern over my absence from school and sought to encourage me. Frustrated, I let out a few curse words and told him to leave me alone. Undeterred, he shared a story about a time when his mother had embarrassed him, and I found myself starting to listen. His words began to resonate with me. Education held significant value for him, and he promised that if I returned to school, he would be my friend. I replied that I would consider it before diving back into the lake to swim home.

I reflected on everything he said, and the most significant statement that resonated with me than, and even now, is his advice: "Don't let anyone take away your education." As the only child in my family to remain in school, I dreamed of graduating. It was an achievement I believed would finally earn me recognition from my family, as no one had completed their education before me. I longed to make them proud. Eventually, I returned to school, and he kept his promise. He accompanied me to the bus stop, checked in on me throughout the day, and we rode the bus home together. I soon faded into the background once more, going unnoticed for a while.

As I previously mentioned, I had transformed into an angry child. It became essential for me to process this situation with my therapist, Noel, especially when I found myself stuck in my writing. I carried a secret, hidden in the 'black' spot of my heart, that I had never shared with anyone. Confronting this lie, which I had been telling myself for nearly 50 years, created internal friction. I have developed a strong, trusting relationship with my therapist, feeling comfortable discussing anything with her except this particular issue. After considerable reflection and comforting my inner child, I finally found the courage to reveal this secret during one therapy session.

I had established rules that were integral to my vows and lifestyle. Our actions were confined to the family unit. One day, when I was nearly 16, my mother deeply hurt me with her words, prompting me to respond with a few choice words of my own. I was seething with anger, felt as if I were about to erupt like a volcano, overwhelmed by my pent-up emotions. In that moment, I noticed a gun lying nearby. Although I had little to no experience with firearms having only observed others being shoot I was consumed by rage. I spotted my mother on the front porch, and though I cannot recall who else was present, I impulsively picked up the gun, envisioning the unthinkable act of shooting her. My anger felt as if it were boiling over. Before I realized it, I had cocked the gun and pulled the trigger in her direction.

I missed her, yet my actions did not go unnoticed. I was ambushed and beaten to the ground, shamed by the realization that I had done something terribly wrong. I could hardly breathe as I tasted the metallic tang of blood running down my throat. When I regained consciousness, I found myself back in my cage, aching and sore, overwhelmed by the stench of my own blood. As I began to respond to my surroundings, I was spit on. Each kick against the cage sent shooting pains coursing through my body. My nutrition deteriorated to the point of consuming spoiled food and water. I lost track of the days spent in that place, but it felt longer than usual. I was overwhelmed with remorse for attempting to harm my mother, the most sacred vow of all: to never hurt fellow members of our coven.

I have kept that a secret forever, feeling ashamed and numb from my actions. I have never allowed myself to experience that level of anger again, as I feared that unleashing the fire of my rage would destroy those around me. The thought terrified me. Instead, I retreated into sadness, a more familiar and safer emotion, fully aware of the havoc I had wreaked within my family.

Journaling

What I have been thinking about, my mom would never hurt me to death because my soulmate would be very angry and I don't know if that's a plus or minus. So many times I wished my soulmate would leave me so my mom would be able to get rid of me. The only reason I am alive today is because of my soulmate and my mom told me that. This is how it was and her talk was unintelligible and inaudible. I hate your stupid ass. I am happy my soulmate loved me but see today how it was just a game. My soulmate would always save me and wanted me. My mom hit me on the back with belts until I would bleed and she would make noises.

Chapter 7

> *"Being in a state of denial is a universally human response to situations which threaten to overwhelm. People who were abused as children sometimes carry their denial like precious cargo without a port of destination. It enabled us to survive our childhood experiences, and often we still live in survival mode decades beyond the actual abuse. We protect ourselves to excess because we learned abruptly and painfully that no one else would."*
>
> *Sarah E. Olson*

A couple of months later, my friend David and I were walking home from the bus stop. David had honored his promise to me for nearly four years. He was my best friend, someone with whom I could share anything permissible school, neighborhood happenings, and his life with his mom. Mostly, we just talked and spent a lot of time swimming together. I felt like a carefree child in his presence.

Our neighborhood had a family that built a platform swing, which all the local kids enjoyed. It had a rope hanging down, and we would swing out over the lake. Those were joyful times, filled with sweet memories of laughter and camaraderie with the other kids.

One day, as David and I made our way home, I noticed my brother sitting on the porch, but I paid little attention to his presence. Suddenly, I saw David slump down before me, blood trickling from his face. In shock, I looked up to find my brother holding a gun, having just shot David. I fell to my knees, desperately trying to lift him. I screamed his name, but he was lifeless, dead. My brother appeared at that moment, and I unleashed my fury upon his chest, crying out, "Why? Why?" His only response was, "I didn't miss," a chilling reference to the day I had shot at our mother. I was left dumbstruck, watching David bleed while my brother laughed at my despair. Overwhelmed, I ran and ran, eventually finding myself at the downtown lake park.

As I sat on a park bench, recovering from my run, I looked down to see David's blood smearing across my clothes. Overwhelmed with grief, I was in no condition to cope. Passersby began to approach, asking if I was alright, but I couldn't regain my composure. The traumatic events replayed in my mind, causing me to spiral into despair once more. I kept repeating, "My brother killed my friend, my brother killed my friend." A crowd had gathered around me, and someone discreetly offered me a couple pills to help calm my racing thoughts.

Gradually, I started to calm down and reflect on my circumstances. I realized I couldn't return home. Fear gripped me. I was uncertain about David's fate. And what about the well-being of his mother? She was now left alone to fend for herself. Did she hold me responsible? Where was my brother? What was I going to do next? I felt an overwhelming urge to cleanse myself of David's blood. I plunged into the lake, consumed by a profound disgust for life and my family. I scrubbed my skin relentlessly, desperate to wash away not just the physical remnants, but also the years of pain that clung to me. As I emerged from the water, I felt a sense of cleanliness washing over me, though it was only skin-deep. A woman awaited my arrival, holding a set of clothes. I was shivering, both physically and emotionally.

That evening, I discovered the stories of the people around me. They were homeless, residing in the park, yet they showed remarkable kindness. On my first night, they offered me a pallet beneath a bench and assured me they would protect me from those who harass park dwellers. I laid down, but sleep eluded me. I missed David and was anxious about what was happening back home. Still, I felt a reluctance to return. Where could I go? I resolved to find answers in the light of the following day.

I must have dozed off for a while because when I finally woke up, it was morning. The people I encountered last night were bustling around me, tidying up to start their day. I walked around the lake, still in a state of shock over David's death. Thoughts of my brother filled my mind, accompanied by a surge of anger. I wondered if my mother was upset with him and wished for my return so she could offer me comfort. As the day progressed, my thoughts became increasingly conflicted. Despite my turmoil, the people around the lake were kind to me, even directing me to a church that provided brown bag lunches.

As I reflected on my past, vivid memories of my younger years spent in the station wagon flooded my mind, particularly the times I was involved in transporting the homeless to a grim fate. *It wasn't until I began writing about these experiences that I recognized the internal conflict I was grappling with. I have dedicated considerable time to therapy, striving to understand why I felt so trapped in this situation. Today, my therapist guided me in unraveling this conflict, enabling me to finally move forward. I revisited my earlier writings and came across a poignant statement: "I made eye contact with the man whenever I could, hoping to convey through my gaze that I was not part of the situation. I wished he noticed my blue eyes."*

This thought lingered in my mind as I observed the homeless noticing my eyes. They affectionately referred to me as "little one" and cherished my "crystal blue" eyes. They took exceptional care of me, ensuring I had enough to eat and provided the necessary medication to prevent withdrawal. This small park had transformed into my home, and I soon came to realize that I was enveloped in love. Was this what it felt like? Perhaps my silent pleas to the homeless had resonated, and I finally experienced unconditional love. I cherished this feeling and began to thrive in it.

During therapy, I was able to articulate the emotions of being loved, feelings that perhaps stemmed from one of the most tragic events of my early years, which echoed into my later life, the death of David. It marked the birth of a new life within me. I finally tasted what I had been searching for all my life, discovering it among the homeless individuals who became my family.

Education had always been paramount to David. Was I still planning to pursue it? As a junior in high school, I stood on the cusp of becoming a senior. David and I often discussed our upcoming senior year, and he was genuinely excited about it. However, with his absence, I found myself questioning whether it still held the same significance for me. Perhaps it was about seeking my family's approval. Maybe they will attend my graduation. I decided to speak with my school counselor. When I met with her, I inquired about my return to school, and she welcomed me. We also talked about the classes I had missed, and she permitted me to take electives instead of core courses since I was so far behind. I lived in the park and attended school, and I felt a renewed sense of purpose. It's funny how life chan   ges when you have people who believe in you, my family of choice.

When I first moved to the park, I inquired about the availability of a bed at the Young Woman's Community Center. Unfortunately, there were no beds available, and that was when the park became my only option. I checked once a week to see if anything had opened, and after 30 days in the park, a room finally became available. Now that I was in school, this placement made sense. I could bathe and have clean clothes. Although it was sad to leave my friends, they were just one street away from my new room.

It was a relief to finally sleep in a bed without the fear of anyone intruding. I could enjoy baths in peace, with the door securely closed. Although I had only a few clothes, I appreciated having a designated space for them, and the community laundry room allowed me to keep my belongings clean.

Every day after school, I would visit my friends, and their excitement for my newfound freedom was unmistakable. I was thriving academically, fueled by a strong determination to complete my studies and graduate. On weekends, I spent time at the park, observing the dynamics of other people and families. It captivated me.

The arrangement I had did not endure for long, however. One day, after returning home from the park, I discovered a note on my door instructing me to see my counselor. In my naivety, unaware of what room checks involved, they uncovered alcohol and some pills in my room. To me, this was a normal occurrence.

I was given just four hours to vacate my safe haven. Despite my affection for the park and the people there, I was reluctant to return.

What was I to do? I pleaded with the counselor for another chance, but they turned me down, citing a lengthy wait-list. Was my placement in my first safe space contingent upon that wait list? I felt like such a fool. I loathed myself, and all the happiness I had experienced seemed to vanish.

To be completely honest, it was incredibly challenging to attend school while living in the park. I struggled to maintain proper hygiene, often going without bathing, and my clothes were perpetually dirty. My inability to care for myself led to painful reminders of my insecurities, especially when the kids used to tease me about my 'green teeth.'

Completing homework became nearly impossible in such conditions; it required immense focus and the limited daylight made concentration difficult. I recognized that my struggles stemmed from having the alcohol and drugs in my room, which had once merely kept me alive but was now robbing me of the very opportunities I needed to succeed.

I faced two choices: remain in the park or return to my family of origin, the coven. Once someone leaves, reentry becomes exceedingly challenging. You become a greater threat, having violated all the vows and commitments you once made. Ultimately, I had no one to blame but myself. I would have to re-engage with my soulmate and prove myself to everyone, however they saw fit. I miss my family, even with all the hate and abuse, it was familiar. I chose not to make any decisions that day. Instead, I went to the park and revisited the experience of living homeless.

With the newfound comfort of having a room for myself, my perspective had shifted. I found myself sleeping under my bench once more, and when I awoke the next morning, the rain was pouring down. The cold rain chilled me to the bone, and I overheard others discussing preparations for the impending cold weather. I was already freezing, lacking even a sheet to shield me from the rain. Cold was something I had always despised, and it had been a constant companion throughout my life. Struggling through the rainy day, I resolved to make my way home again. As I retraced the same route I had taken a month and a half earlier, thoughts of David and my brother flooded my mind. Where was my brother? What would I do if

I encountered him? A sense of fear gripped me at the thought of both possibilities, but with colder weather approaching, my desire to escape the chill grew stronger.

Chapter 8

I stood at the door, drenched and shivering, anxiously awaiting who would answer. The evening was dark, but the lights were on, indicating that someone was home. Finally, my older sister opened the door and saw me standing there. I asked if I could come in, but she said she needed to check with our mother first. After a moment, she returned with the news that I could only enter as far as the living room until I was searched. My mother came in to inspect me and found me clean. I requested a bath to warm up, but she denied my plea. Instead, I was allowed to sleep on the couch in my wet clothes, without any extra bedding, until the entire coven could meet with me. That night, though I froze, I managed to get some sleep.

The following morning, my mother announced that the group meeting would take place at noon. She finally allowed me to take a bath and offered me a cup of coffee. However, she never mentioned David or expressed any sympathy for his death. I suspected that the cup of coffee was intended as a "peace offering." To my surprise, she had added whiskey, which helped warm me up.

As noon approached, I began to feel dizzy. I realized she had mixed something else into my coffee, as I could barely stand while walking to the room. I found myself grappling with conflicting emotions, having experienced genuine affection from those who had so little. Could I truly return to the way things were before?

When I reached the ritual room, everyone was already there. Even my brother, whom I hadn't seen since David's death, was present. I tried to confront him, to "give him what he deserved," but I was becoming groggier and had to sit down. It felt as though I was under the influence of Somas, a muscle relaxer. I felt like slime and couldn't gain control of my body. Before I knew it, I was on the floor, barely able to comprehend what was happening. My soulmate approached me, removed my clothes, and promptly got on top of me. I felt sick to my stomach, and a sense of evil surged back into my body. I passed out before he finished. In a twisted way, I felt that drugging me was a blessing because when I woke up, I was in excruciating pain. I found myself in my cage, naked, the confines feeling increasingly small. I had to shift my position to find some comfort.

As I immersed myself in that moment, I felt a sensation akin to a crunching feeling deep within. I urged my sister to share what had transpired. She revealed that every person, regardless of gender, had been involved with me, including my mother, who had placed snake eggs inside me after everything had concluded. Snake eggs... My sister explained that they would restore all that I had left behind, allowing it to become a part of me once more. A wild feeling of trepidation surged through me as I sensed the crunch of the snake eggs within.

Once again, I found myself contemplating whether I could return to this lifestyle. I had experienced love and affection, yet I questioned my choices. Fully immersed in the coven, I realized there was no turning back.

After a few days, thoughts of school began to resurface, and I returned just three days after coming home. It felt rewarding to be back at school, knowing I was honoring my commitment to David. I also started working at TG&Y, where I sold fabric in the sewing department. Since I was taking Home Economics as an elective, I began learning to make my own clothes. I quickly became a skilled seamstress, even receiving requests to create outfits for the mannequins.

While I enjoyed the distraction of work, it became apparent that my family noticed I was also attending school when I claimed to be working. I needed to find a different way to conceal my education. I was driven by my determination to graduate. By this point, I was a senior and eagerly anticipated my graduation. I started staying in people's backyards by the lake, allowing me to attend school without my family noticing. Additionally, I began saving money for a car.

I managed to take the bus to school without anyone noticing my departure, as I would leave through the backyard of my neighbors. After school, I would head straight to work, and this arrangement suited me well. Gradually, I found myself spending less time at home. I would return from work, complete my homework, and as night fell, I would leave the house again. I had established a safe place to sleep and even sneaked out a blanket to keep warm during the night. This arrangement worked well for several months. If I continued to fulfill my obligations at home and earn my keep, no one mentioned the time I was away.

As graduation approached, I received invitations to send out. About a week before the ceremony, I distributed invitations to my family, hoping to see them there to support me. However, I faced consequences for lying to my mother about continuing my education. Despite this, my feelings for David motivated me to complete my studies. Yes, I graduated! I could feel David's spirit, sharing in my joy. On graduation night, as I walked across the stage, I felt immense gratitude for David's influence in my life. After the ceremony, I looked around for some family members, but there were none. My soulmate was not even there after telling me he was coming. I felt deep sadness and disappointment. Nevertheless, I had graduated and fulfilled a commitment that was not meant to elicit a negative response.

Now that school is over, I could dedicate more time to my work. I increased my hours and managed to buy myself an affordable car. Having transportation provided me with a newfound sense of independence. I spent less time at home and was able to explore more.

One day, I visited the park and shared my achievements with my homeless friends. They were incredibly proud of me, embracing me warmly, and we expressed our gratitude to David, who had initially drawn me to the park. After leaving, I went to work, only to discover that I had been fired for theft. While saving for my car, I had hoarded my paychecks to reach this goal. In my desperation, I began stealing female hygiene products from the store, consumed by my focus on saving money. I felt immense guilt for my actions and reluctantly left the store that day.

I found myself without gas money, which forced me to stay home more often and led to a deeper commitment to "earning my keep." The attic, still a part of the house, became the primary setting for most of my business activities. I often regretted the decision I had made. I began to wonder if I could truly return to the way things were before. Thoughts of the snake eggs resurfaced, reminding me of how they had drawn me back into this predicament. It felt as though they were once again living within me. Although I had never mentioned it before, when I was given two spirit guides, names omitted, at a young age, their voices had faded while I was happily living in the park, but now they had returned with full force.

I found myself grappling with old thoughts that urged me to retreat and find solace with my family. However, my family seemed increasingly volatile, even resorting to the senseless killing of innocent animals around us. I felt deep resentment towards my life and regretted my return. I longed for the love and acceptance I once experienced.

One day, while my brother and I were home alone, I felt a surge of anger towards him. I missed David profoundly and was frustrated that my brother faced no repercussions for his actions. In a moment of rage, I attacked him biting, scratching, and kicking. It took just one blow for me to realize I could not overpower him. I retreated, as my spirit guide advised. I continued to live with my family for four years, participating in their worship and striving to remain focused on them.

During this time, I took a babysitting job and saved every penny I earned. I began to contemplate leaving once more. In my desperation, I started stealing money from my clients, withholding some of my earnings from my mother, especially the tips.

I started visiting bars at night, since I had the freedom to do so. I met a variety of people and became completely immersed in the nightlife. One particular guy caught my attention; he was an excellent dancer, and I loved dancing. He invited me to lunch, and I happily accepted. I confided in my sister about him and our lunch date, believing she would keep it a secret. Although she expressed her disapproval, she promised to keep my secret safe. However, everything changed when my mother mentioned that a friend had seen me at a sandwich shop with someone. My sister confirmed this to our mother, and the following night, as I was leaving the bar, I found myself in a frightening situation. I pressed the brakes in my car, but it wouldn't stop! Fortunately, I remembered the emergency brake, pulled it, and managed to halt the vehicle. I walked back to the bar and asked a friend to come look at it. My brake lines were cut. Intentionally, he suspected.

What I discovered at home was alarming; my soulmate was extremely angry with me and had expressed a desire to see me dead. He envisioned my car crashing on the many hills where I lived, imagining that it would appear like an accident with no evidence left behind. This marked the beginning of my downfall with him. He was fed up with me, and I began completely rejecting him. I felt as though I had only days to live, given his feelings. My mother even became involved, threatening me with a gun held to my head. With only $1,000 saved, I decided it was time to escape. I kept my plans secret, not even informing the family I babysat for. I was already in a precarious situation with them, having developed an interest in their toddler boy. Although nothing inappropriate occurred with the boy, my upbringing left me confused about boundaries.

I had found myself grappling with a profound question: to live or to die. I made the decision to live. If I stayed, I would face consequences. I had already experienced a brush with death. Distracted, I realized I had disrupted a ritualistic ceremony, and I sensed that my time was running out. As I grew older and more independent, I understood that my family had become entangled in the allure of firearms. I had faced a gun held to my head and managed to escape, but I questioned how long that escape would last. I longed to break free from my soulmate, yearning for happiness.

I knew it was crucial to leave, especially for my own safety. I began to pack my belongings into my car, taking only what would fit. No one seemed to notice my preparations, and one evening, I got into my car and drove away.

Chapter 9

The only path to freedom was to leave. I was 22 years old. I crafted my plan and packed my car, fully aware that the day to leave had arrived, bringing with it a weight of consequences. If I tried to get away and I got caught, the question would not be if I would die. It would be how they chose to eliminate me. But, the fear of leaving had become less than the fear of staying, and I did what I had to do.

I drove down to the interstate. Panic surged through me every time a car followed closely behind. I felt like a frightened little girl lost in a vast world. The hardest part was the guilt of knowing they had been grooming my little niece to take someone's place. That thought pierced my heart. She was the oldest niece, in her teens, the daughter of my sister. I had been watching how they began including her in their practices and had assigned her a "mentor" to teach her the ins and outs of our religion. Knowing and seeing all of this, I had to just push those emotions away because I could no longer endure the lifestyle I was living.

Journaling

The last gift I received was freedom from my family of origin. It comes up on emotion code as grief 2 times but I cannot reconcile it as grief as I had so many mixed feelings leaving.

Possibly some grief over my niece taking my place in the coven or so many other things. I could be grieving over a lot I have tucked away. Really been working on that emotion and looking at where the root is coming from. I struggle with grief a lot but I have come so far, why do I still need to feel grief? What am I missing? Why can't I build myself up? Why do I need confirmation from people in my life today. I have to get it from within.

With a sense of determination, I drove west, embarking on a journey to an unfamiliar and unknown destination. Armed with $1000.00 in cash and my car packed with all my belongings, I was filled with a blend of excitement and anxiety. It felt as though I were a child, exploring a new world brimming with wonders. I began to ponder, "How far could I go with $1000? Could I find a place to call home? How would I know where to settle?"

My nerves started to overwhelm me. It was dark outside, I didn't know where I was going. I had no one to help guide me but I thought I could do this, finally. Among the things I did not think about was the drugs. Did I have enough? When I get somewhere, then what? Are my Spirit Guides still around to help me? I didn't know all these answers, and I felt like the child I once had been – confused, fearful and alone.

I drove through the night and into the following day, completely unaware of my destination or what I was looking for. I passed through numerous cities but ultimately decided to stop in one. I spent three days there, encountering several mishaps along the way. I struggled to find anyone at the bars who had the substances I craved. While driving down the interstate, a pebble kicked up from a truck and cracked my windshield. I also realized that $1000.00 didn't last long at all. I was feeling uncomfortable in that city; it just didn't fit me. I decided to leave and continued my journey westward.

My mind started to play tricks on me, and I found myself depending on my spirit guides to lead me to new destinations. I also began to question my choice to leave. My guides made it abundantly clear that returning was not an option; doing so would surely lead to my demise. I couldn't shake the thoughts of what I had done to my niece and the difficult situation I had placed her in. The guilt and shame were consuming me from the inside out.

I found myself compelled to behave like an adult, yet deep down, I never truly felt that way. I now realize I was still navigating life with a child's perspective, ill-equipped for the trials that awaited me in the coming three years. But I was doing the best I could with what I had, not knowing any better way. It was a haunting experience, albeit a different kind of nightmare. I had traded the trauma that was going to kill me for a trauma I didn't know.

My funds dwindled quickly. In my mind, it felt like I left with fortune. However, after accounting for the unexpected travel expenses, I found myself broke. I finally found a city that felt like it could be my new home. I discovered a country/western bar and met people who could support me in my habits. I loved to dance, so I had a way to meet people there. Uncertain of my next steps and the money situation, I was haunted by the thought of returning home. I feared failure once more, and I recognized that my only barrier to success was money. That was the one thing that I absolutely had to have to survive. So, I found a way to survive.

Journaling

Such a panicked feeling to run. My anxiety gets
  going and I am so tempted to try to escape my
head. I remember the feelings of driving away.
What power it gave me. I was so free and no one
– no turning back. I just need to vanish. The
  images, the voices behind me, I startle a lot.
I do not know who is out to get me anymore. I
  wish I could vocalize the image in my head.
They are covering me like slime. They seep and
slide and I stink. My hair is so messed up. I
  have lots of heads, they are green. Too many
men. There's to many men. Theirs to many, I
still am sore. But another one slimes me. I am
so weak. I am so small. I am so broken and I
fall down. And they step on my back to keep me
down. It really hurts a lot but Dr. G is there
  with the pills. Mom says the men love little
girls and they give her money and that's a head
of mine.

I began to go home with men from the bar, who took care of me. I needed to earn money, and I knew exactly how to achieve that. I wouldn't have to relinquish control; it would be my money. No one else would be getting it, just me. To make ends meet, I resorted to prostitution. This was a very familiar and "safe" occupation for me. I feel like as a woman I had no value and no control over my life. This allowed me to have money which offered me some sense of control.

Many men offered to take care of me and manage the business aspect, but I realized I was exhausted of people having control over me. I chose to go solo. I learned about where to hang. I learned about hotels and about "in calls" and 'out calls". I knew all the wordings, how to word things so you don't get arrested. I kind of played a trick on myself when I called it being a "call girl" because I felt so sophisticated. After all, I wasn't out turning tricks on the streets. But I knew in my heart I was turning tricks.

I would go to people's houses, and I didn't think anything of it when I'd walk in, and they'd walk in and they'd deadbolt the door. Anything could have happened to me. Anything. I remember getting raped a lot. Like, men would rip off my clothes and do whatever they wanted. It got to the point where I didn't really care anymore. I wasn't very content with how I was living, but I tried to convince myself that I didn't care. So, I just got used to it and kept going.

The most significant takeaway from that time is that I survived. I endured the lifestyle and acquired some sense of stability, although it was fragile. It was better than what I had left, which isn't saying much. I was still trapped; however, this was a cage of my choosing. I had the ability to leave when the time was right.

I started getting my life in order, I rented a house, secured a "real" job, and spent my nights at the bar, surrounded by friends. I gained access to the VIP section and danced on tables throughout those three years. Life was enjoyable. I was often under the influence, yet I performed well at work. My family was a distant thought, and I was creating my own hell on earth. From the outside it appeared that I had succeeded in my escape.

However, little had changed within me. My soulmate had implanted valuable lessons, and I was thriving. My success at this point was based on his influence on me, both in bed and out of bed. His strong presence hovered near me, even if he wasn't physically present.

During this period, I now see that I hadn't acquired many essential adult life skills, as I was still deeply influenced by my upbringing. I adhered to the principles instilled in me, sometimes even participating in ritualistic events. I often questioned whether I had truly left my past behind or merely changed my surroundings.

At some point, I took a job as an appointment setter for a hospital. It was such an adjustment when it came to payday, and thinking about the money I was missing out on with my other job. So, I incorporated both, not to the extent that I had, but just to supplement my income. I guess you could say I stayed at that job part-time.

After several weeks at my new job, my boss approached me. I had had many crying spells on the job and was late often, but I felt like I had my drinking under control. She stated she had concerns for me and I was still in a probationary period. I knew "probation" as a legal term but never a work term. She explained they had a chance to terminate me if I didn't work out.

She suggested I see a psychologist and get checked out to see if medication would help. She explained to me about having insurance soon and recommended a doctor for me. So, I started seeing him and he began prescribing pills for me. Having used pills in the past to deaden my emotions, this seemed a normal solution to me.

I talked with him about what my job was saying about my performance, and he helped me understand work ethics. I was seeing him once a month. I was learning that jobs had rules, and I was not a rule follower, yes, my job was in jeopardy. He was aware of my suicidal thoughts and proposed a contract: I was to call him if I ever felt suicidal. I found the idea of a contract perplexing; I couldn't imagine reaching out for help in that state.

One night, after returning home from work, I was taken aback when someone knocked on my door. Living on a busy road, I was accustomed to seeing many people around. When I opened the door, I found my sister standing there with her four children. I was stunned but welcomed them inside, only to be shocked by the disheveled state of the children. To this day, I still wonder how she managed to find my address. She expressed her desire to start anew. I remembered my desperation to escape, and I knew how much I wanted someone to be there to help me.

But her children had never enrolled in school, had lice in their hair, and were unkempt. They wore the only clothes they had on their backs. Overwhelmed with emotion, I realized that I had once been in a similar situation to the children. The oldest had blue eyes! I felt a strong urge to help them and create a better life for them. I realize now that I was trying to save myself by saving them. I was looking for some existential balance to win a victory over my past.

After navigating through a lot of bureaucratic hurdles, I managed to get them enrolled in school. My sister struggled with heavy drinking and drug use, but she had a big enough supply for both of us, and she shared. Although I reduced my visits to bars, I continued my side business since she was not working.

About a week later, she started receiving phone calls from my family. I did not want to have contact with them. My sister did not understand. In a moment of anger, she violently threw me by my hair when I refused to speak to our mother. This resulted in a concussion of sorts. During her stay, I did speak with my soulmate over the phone, because I missed him terribly. I felt as though I was caught between two worlds, and my internal struggle resurfaced. I had been out of the family for three years and somehow, I thought speaking with him might give me some kind of reassurance.

Frequent arguments erupted with my sister. The primary reason was her neglecting the children while I worked. The language these babies used were the same words I had learned at an early age. I felt my sister sincerely wanted a life change but, just like me, she feared the consequences.

The children were very stoic in their everyday activities, and I recognized a lot of me in them at this age. They appeared to be motivated not by joy and interest, but by the avoidance of consequences.

One day, I finally reached my breaking point. I returned home to find the baby alone, the older kids still at school, and my sister nowhere in sight. That night, while bathing the kids and hearing them cry for their mom, I had no explanation for them. It tore my very soul to hear these children living some of my darkest childhood fears.

The following day she returned, and I cannot even begin to describe the chaos that ensued. I found myself regressing to my childhood, reliving the trauma I had experienced. She seemed to have no attachment to her children, taking care of her needs before theirs. My family had turned her into my mother!

She was thrashing words at me, many that I heard as a child. She knew my hot spots and didn't hesitate to inflict pain on me by using my past against me. I exploded inside of myself. In that moment, I made the difficult decision to contact OCS and report my sister. Maybe it was for me in my head, but at that point I wanted help for these children.

The following day, after work, I found a note on my door addressed to my sister. OCS had received a report and had come to investigate, but no one was home. The note requested that she call and make an appointment for them to meet. I was dumbfounded at how incredibly naive OCS must be to think my sister would actually invite them back to have a chat. This was worse than when Family Services showed up and missed everything at my house when I was a child. It left a deep emptiness in the pit of my stomach.

At some point during the night, my sister and her children left. She did not take any of their belongings, abandoning all their clothes and everything I had tried to do for them. I felt powerless to save them. I had lost this battle, and the defeat was demoralizing.

The next day at work, I was distraught with all the memories, images and harm these children would face. I had fought to save the child I was with these children, and I failed miserably. The glimmer of hope I provided them was snuffed out in a mere 24 hours.

Chapter 10

> *"Here is the test to find whether your mission on Earth is finished: if you're alive, it isn't."*
>
> *Richard Bach*

As I sat at my desk, I realized that if I got up and drove my car, I would crash into a tree. I can, even to this day, feel that feeling. I was empty, alone, powerless, exposed and shamed. I am not sure what saved me that day, but I called my psychologist and asked for help. That silly contract I made with him actually worked!

I felt like a drowned puppy exhausted, defeated, and terrified. I longed for an escape. That day in February 1985, I was admitted to the psychiatric ward of the hospital, broken, dejected and crushed. I was both hopeless and helpless. I was done. I did my best and it was not good enough. My psychologist made a visit, saw the shape I was in, and confirmed I needed to be there. During my time there, they conducted numerous tests on me. I vividly recall the "blot" test, where everything appeared as blood and bloody figures. I was counseled by someone who worked on the unit, and I attended groups. I was on many medications and scarcely remember much of that stay. My mind was so confused, and they kept asking me all kinds of questions. I didn't feel safe enough to tell them my real story. I had learned as a child that I was not allowed to talk about my family. I was still driven by that invisible loyalty that had a strangle hold on my existence.

There was a man in the unit who would jump up in a window and proclaim he was Christ Jesus, and we would go round and round because I claimed I was Satan's child. I'm sure it was quite the spectacle for the staff and other patients. The tragedy of the situation was we both believed what we were saying.

I was involved in Art Therapy in the unit, and I started feeling safe with the therapist. She loved everything I did, told me I was good, and that she was very proud of me. She would put my art on display for others to see. After doctor visits and therapy, I would talk to her, and she would help me sort out my brain after the sessions. She helped me see what false messages and true messages were. She provided healthy guidance and provided a level of sincere concern that I sorely lacked in my life. The seed of life inside me was experiencing water for the first time.

After three months, they considered discharging me. I had settled into a routine in that environment; it felt safe, and I could communicate my medication needs to my psychiatrist who complied with my requests. During my outings, I would often buy over-the-counter medicine which, when consumed in large quantities, would give me a buzz. I would sneak out during shift changes to the nearby 7-Eleven to purchase beer and hide it under my bed in an ice cooler. Back then, security was not as strict as it is now. The prospect of discharge brought forth all my fears, and I found myself contemplating suicide once more. I had finally found a somewhat threat-free environment and the thought of leaving it sent chills through my inmost being.

With nowhere to go and no family to turn to, I would gaze out of the 7th floor window, struggling to understand how life functioned. I had lost everything I had during that stay in the hospital. My car had been repossessed. I felt utterly destitute. I began acting out, as this was what I had learned. When the suicidal thoughts returned, I was scared to death but did not know how to explain it to people in words. I had not spoken of my past, and I really wanted to be the boy in the window who identified as Christ Jesus.

They didn't force him to do group therapy or anything. They did not ask him questions like they did me. I tried to understand the differences between him and I, and maybe it was that he talked about being Jesus in group and was very communicative, and I remained in my shell, not talking.

No one understood I could not get my brain to work because I could not comprehend, much less communicate, what had happened to me at this point. I didn't have the words or the comprehension to describe my past. I was still living my trauma – stuck in fight, flight or freeze. My emotions and survival skills were in control and there was no way I could rationally process how I got in this state of mind. And even if I did, would they even believe me, or would they think I was making everything up?

I worked well with helping other people during group. They seemed more worthy than me. I had always found value in helping others but never asked for help myself. The other patients had family that came to see them and encouraged them, while I sat there and played Solitaire by myself. I don't think the staff would have known what to do if MY family had shown up.

Instead of discharging me, the treatment team decided to keep me and focus on teaching me life skills. My art therapist began teaching me about hygiene, how to read directions if I wanted to make anything to eat, and she even allowed me to make macaroni and cheese several times. These were some of the simple building blocks to life that I had been denied. We talked about what emotions were and began putting words to them.

Between my medication increases and what I had brought into the hospital, I managed to stay relatively buzzed during my stay. I spent another three months in the unit, engaging in arts and crafts, life skills, and enjoying no responsibilities. All my meals were provided for me. Yet, it was challenging to accept my situation. I felt safe, but I was burdened by the lack of pressure to earn my keep.

One day, a search of my room revealed all my OTC medications, empty beer bottles, and burned sheets from smoking while falling asleep with lit cigarettes. As a result, I was placed in lockdown and confined to a room with only a bed. It was the hospital's version of a cage, although it was much more comfortable than the thin metal of a dog cage. I experienced flashbacks of looking at my mother through the small window when she was in lockdown; I felt a deep connection to her. Was I becoming her?

The nurse informed me that if I behaved, they might show leniency. My interpretation of being good involved sitting in a corner and working on a puzzle all night, ensuring I didn't disturb anyone. They mentioned that the coroner would arrive in the morning to determine the next steps regarding my situation. They proposed the possibility of admitting me to the state psychiatric hospital for a year.

On August 5, 1985, the coroner arrived to meet with me. He reviewed my case and indicated it was time to move forward. My insurance was about to expire, and he believed the best option at that moment was what the nurses had suggested: a year at the state hospital. I was acutely aware that if I entered a hospital for a year, I would likely be institutionalized for the rest of my life. Just like I had done in the hospital, I would adapt to life within the facility, feel safe, and would no longer have to navigate the challenges of survival. But I would also be labeled as mentally ill. The thought of this choice terrified me; it felt like the ultimate defeat after enduring so much.

As if in the fog of a dream, words I had never anticipated saying escaped my lips. I confessed to the coroner that I needed help with my alcohol and drug use. I must have heard it from somewhere, or maybe I remembered my sister and knew I was doing as much as her when she was living with me. I thought that about her and was thinking the same about myself. Maybe there was some other power driving me in this direction. I honestly don't know. Whatever the source, I finally asked for help for myself. I was in uncharted territory.

The coroner reassured me, saying, "As long as you are willing to seek help, you are not commit-table." When he asked if I wanted to enter treatment, I responded affirmatively. I was transferred to the Substance Abuse Unit that day and established my sobriety, going cold turkey on August 6, 1985.

Chapter 11

> *Your unhealthy habits were just survival mechanisms that you held onto to protect yourself. You aren't trying to be self destructive! Your brain is just telling you that danger is imminent so you prepare accordingly. But you just need to slowly build new, healthy habits because you aren't in danger anymore.*
>
> *Unknown*

The first five days of treatment were marked by a challenging detox from all medications, both prescription and over the counter. My psychiatrist had "fired" me and now I had a new doctor, a doctor that knew about addiction. Having used substances throughout my life, the detox process proved to be incredibly difficult. At times it was torturous, but looking back it was worth the pain to become drug-free.

By Day 6, I began to awaken to the true essence of treatment. I had made countless choices throughout my life without fully grasping their implications. I only knew that this path had to be better than the one I was on. Completely abstaining from drugs was not something I had anticipated, and the subsequent 30 days were tough.

People interacted with me, but I did not know what their motive was. I had learned to be wary of anyone who was being nice to me without an obvious motive. People always have a motive.

I wrapped myself in a blanket for comfort, with only my blue eyes visible during my time in treatment. I attended AA meetings where others reached out to touch and hug me, which I shunned them and felt overwhelmed. They had smiles on their faces and I truly did not know how to respond. I had a roommate who completed her treatment before I did; she visited me and shockingly brought a joint along. I was astounded that she would place me in such a precarious position after seeing me endure the pain of detoxing. I knew the pains of recovering again far outweighed the initial high I would get. I understand now that she was trying to help me the only way she knew how, but I didn't need that. Her actions significantly influenced my resolve to remain sober.

Group therapy on this unit felt entirely different than on the psych floor. It was a space where we could share our past experiences while contemplating our present circumstances and future aspirations. Despite the eagerness of others to share their stories, I found myself remaining silent, reluctant to voice my own. I contributed just enough feedback to blend in. Once again, I didn't have the capacity at that time to delve into everything. But I did learn what I needed to learn to stay clean. And I saw the process that was working for the other patients on the unit.

During treatment, we had AA meetings where individuals from outside would come in to facilitate discussions. Their accounts of sobriety outside of treatment intimidated me. They discussed securing employment, attending meetings, finding sponsors, the risk of relapsing, and developing coping mechanisms. Additionally, they spoke about a Higher Power, and some even mentioned God, which made me feel even more isolated. I questioned my ability to participate in this program. My resentment towards God lingered, and I continued to silently recite my vows and pretenses in my mind. Consequently, I withdrew further, keeping my fears and insecurities bottled up inside.

During an AA meeting one day, I was wrapped in my blanket when an older man approached and playfully pinched my toe. Although it was a harmless gesture, I felt a surge of anger at his touch. Surprisingly, he later became a significant figure in my recovery journey and only then he shared that the look I gave him that day inspired him to stay sober for the next six months.

As time passed, I gradually started to connect with others. I began putting things together with a clearer mind and really worked on comprehending Step 1 in AA. I truly did not believe I was powerless over alcohol and drugs. They had saved my life many times, and they saved my brain by protecting it from seeing and registering tragic things in my life. I thought I had very good control over the intake, knowing my body well.

My life was unmanageable, but it was only because I left my family, which was a choice I made. I now see that I blamed the choice that saved my life for making my life unmanageable. My ability to process things was still very skewed by my indoctrination.

With my discharge approaching, we began to discuss my next steps and where I would go from there. The only viable option for me was a halfway house. They explained that it was a sober living environment outside of treatment, accommodating many women in recovery. We would attend AA meetings, take responsibility for securing employment, pay rent, and be expected to maintain sobriety.

After a seven-month stay in a facility, the doctors and staff believed this was the most suitable placement for me. I mean, what else could I do? I was terrified to leave the hospital; it had been the only long-term safe space I had ever known. I felt incredibly alone and undermined by my inability to function in the outside world while sober. I was familiar with one way to earn a living, but I realized I would need to learn new skills. I had learned a lot from my art therapist so maybe I had some hope.

Life in a halfway house revolves around structure and accountability. I did not realize how much I needed these. Structure is the number one enemy of addiction. Addiction is about chaos. Chaos and structure cannot coexist for any length of time. Accountability meant I would be held to a higher standard than what I would convince myself was okay for me.

I had to adhere to a set schedule that includes chores, group meetings, therapy sessions, and educational programs. I realized how undisciplined I was with normal daily activities. The house mother said it would help me develop essential life skills necessary for independent living. Additionally, I had to adhere to curfews and maintain sobriety, with regular drug testing to ensure compliance.

I had a roommate with whom I shared a room, and although I was uncertain about this arrangement, I needed a place to stay. I attended three meetings each day, where discussions often centered around a higher power. Each time the topic arose, I reflected on my own understanding of a higher power, which only deepened my confusion. I became very defiant, starting arguments and bringing my chaos into the house. But at least I was talking about my confusion, rather than letting it boil on the back burner of my brain. I was defending something deep down but was not sure what it was. I had deep conviction that I was dishonoring something that I had a lot of loyalty to. I was discovering a lot in this half-way house.

I also needed to secure a sponsor, but I struggled to find someone who could relate to my perspective. Then the members of the group began to question my interpretation of a higher power. I felt invaded – they were getting too close! This caused me to retreat further into myself rather than engage in the "recovery process".

I found myself questioning my existence once more, wondering if Alcoholics Anonymous was the right path for me. After all, how could I believe in a god that had caused me so much pain? In those early days of recovery, I felt incredibly lost and isolated. I refrained from speaking in meetings and did not participate in the "chip system". I wanted no recognition for my accomplishments. When I sat in meetings and heard of people having 20 and 25 years of sobriety, still sitting in meetings, I pondered if this is needed - a place to feel secure.

I met a friend named David who attended the meetings. He understood my struggles with god and called me every morning to turn my will and my life over to his God for the day. Each night, he would check in to see how God had worked in my life. He showed me you can have fun in sobriety. I spent many nights at the coffee shop, drinking coffee, mixing with other people and interacting by attending conferences. I realized I was having fun. I was part of a group of people! There were people who accepted me just as I was, where I was.

My friendship with David lasted four years. Sadly, David passed away from cirrhosis of the liver. Even so, he had a great impact on my life. I deeply miss his encouragement and laughter.

I was eventually kicked out of the halfway house. I did not meet their expectations and requirements. I experienced feelings of abandonment, unworthiness and shame but felt limited in whom I could confide in, which led to me becoming very withdrawn. I had belonged, and now I was excluded. Once again, I found myself alone with nowhere to go.

That man from the AA meeting in the hospital – the one who pinched my toe - offered me the attic of a vacant house he rented. Having been homeless before, I accepted the attic, which had no electricity. I relied on only a flashlight and my Big Book of Alcoholics Anonymous.

I was very limited in resources, missing my meetings and meeting up with the friends I had made. I had no transportation, still no job, and no sponsor. I had time to contemplate many things in my life, often thinking about my family and old familiar feelings. I was missing my soul mate. I thought he would have had all my answers I needed, but I clung to my sobriety, not ever wanting to feel the pain of detox again. Sometimes it's helpful to have time to sit and process your progress.

A friend of mine offered me a position as a receptionist at his brick masonry company. Excited at the opportunity, I dedicated myself to that job. I learned how to be approachable, how to answer phones and how to relay messages. In return, my friend assisted me in acquiring an affordable car for transportation. I finally had a little money and my own wheels again! Around that time, I had the opportunity to move in with a woman who owned a house. I was starting to carve out my own path and build a future for myself. Things were looking up again.

Eventually, I found a sponsor with whom I could connect. She was an earthy person, deeply in tune with nature, and helped me understand a higher power as something beyond my control. She suggested and understood why I had chosen a doorknob as my higher power. I completed my fourth step (a deep personal inventory) and presented it to her in my fifth step. Although I had not yet sorted out my life, I did my best with her guidance. I still had much healing to do.

Unfortunately, my sponsor passed away before we could delve deeper into my journey. I remember visiting her in the hospital, continuing to talk to her, unwilling to accept her illness or the thought of losing her. She used to talk about how life was not a dressed rehearsal. This is it, and you don't get to go back and change things. Her passing froze my progress and my journey toward recovery, yet I remained sober.

I came to understand that this was my method of maintaining sobriety for many years - I absorbed a wealth of information, but I found myself giving nothing back in return. So, I became a very outward friend to many, helping when they struggled, but still I harbored a bundle of emotions inside of me.

Chapter 12

> *"Healing may not be so much about getting better, as about letting go of everything that isn't you – all of the expectations, all of the beliefs – and becoming who you are."*
>
> *Remen*

My sponsor had been deeply immersed in Native American culture and generously shared her experiences with me. The concept of The Great Spirit captivated my interest, prompting me to explore their culture further after her passing. I encountered a Medicine Man, a Chippewa Indian, with whom I spent considerable time. His stories and insights into Indian culture mesmerized me.

Although he was ten years my senior, he captured my attention, and I affectionately referred to him as Father. Eventually, we married in an Indian ceremony officiated by a medicine woman we had met. We participated in the entire marriage ritual, which included spitting into the fire four times and honoring the traditional medicine wheel. A priest later formalized our union, laying the foundation for our life together. She bestowed upon me an Indian name that I cherish to this day. Together, we traveled to pow-wows and engaged in various Indian rituals.

When my husband was in his "Indian" circle or presenting Indian culture to young children, he thrived. However, upon returning home, he transformed himself into a different person. I felt as though I provoked this change. This isn't unusual for a trauma survivor. I was constantly trying to do everything right to make him happy. I later realized that this, too, was something I learned from my childhood. I thought I could control how he felt. I would often tell him that I would prefer he hit me rather than be silent to me. I wanted some kind of indicator of what I did "wrong" so I could change it in the future. I was always trying to make everything "good". I was so accustomed to this behavior from childhood that I didn't recognize it as wrong.

After a couple of years of marriage, friends began to ask if I had been experiencing abuse. I was taken aback and uncertain how to respond, as I had grown accustomed to the way I was treated. This was my "normal". I had not assumed that having bruises and a couple of black eyes would be noticed by others, but to them it was a clear indication that something was wrong.

My husband had two grown children, one of whom struggled with alcohol addiction. He also had a brain tumor that necessitated surgery. When my stepson failed to meet his father's expectations, he tragically took his own life. My husband's anger spiraled out of control, and during this tumultuous time, a friend named Robin became my steadfast support. She was someone I felt I could trust.

I met Robin and we became quick friends. She faced challenges with her sobriety. Despite our struggles, we connected on a profound level, sharing our past traumas that led us both to seek recovery. Sometimes the right person just appears in your life at the perfect time. We created cherished memories together, including the opening of a coffee shop we named Paradox. Robin also led an all-female band that performed at our cafe, bringing joy and laughter into our lives.

We had a sign with the "8 Paradoxes of Sobriety" hanging in the Paradox Cafe. They are:

1. We surrender to win.
2. We suffer to get well.
3. We give it away to keep it.
4. We die to live.
5. He who loses his life does indeed find it.

6. The more you give, the more you get.
7. The less you think of yourself, the more of a person you become.
8. We can laugh at those who think spirituality is the way of weakness. Paradoxically, it is the way of strength.

I still have that sign today. It holds so many beautiful memories for me.

In moments of fear, when I felt haunted by inner demons, Robin comforted me. My own recovery required focus, and there were times I had to distance myself from her struggles to maintain my sobriety. Yet, she always knew she could return to me for support. She was one of those people I could not see for several weeks and then pick our relationship back up like we were together the whole time.

I attended the Unitarian Universalist Church, a place where many from Alcoholics Anonymous found solace due to its inclusive definition of a Higher Power. After my stepson's suicide, I sought a conversation with the pastor, as I began experiencing flashbacks to my past. There was a need inside me for guidance and confirmation that I, in fact, was being abused. He did confirm the abuse and saw me for several months about my flashbacks.

He called my memories I was having Trauma. While this was a familiar experience for me, I never had a label for it. I did not ask for the things I've been through. And I certainly didn't ask my mind to paint and repaint the pictures back in flashback form. I thought it was just how life was supposed to be. What I learned was Trauma is a mental injury, and our body may react to unconscious memories of significant negative events unknown even to us. Our body subconsciously protects us from future trauma. When I began to get into some sexual trauma, the pastor referred me to a female therapist at a counseling community center. I am thankful for his wisdom.

During this period, I also distanced myself from the church, coming to the unsettling realization that because of their undefined "god" my own mother could be standing beside me and worship the devil. I had not considered that my understanding of a higher power could even encompass the notion of Satan. Various services ignited this discernment within me, yet I remained skeptical until I sought clarity, and the pastor candidly addressed my concerns.

Through this time, my husband became increasingly angry, especially over the death of his son. After reading a note left by my stepson, which expressed that his feelings of inadequacy in meeting his father's expectations led him to take his own life, my husband only got worse. In the aftermath, my husband turned to alcohol and began performing rituals at our fireplace, seeking clarity about his relationship with his son and the circumstances surrounding his tragic demise. Unfortunately, the abuse directed at me intensified. I found myself oddly comfortable with the abuse, far more than I was with the idea of leaving the safety and familiarity of my situation. The pain of staying had not gotten bigger than the fear of leaving, so I stayed.

I was shocked and humiliated when he initiated a divorce. I was emotionally cut to the bone when I was served the papers. Devastated, I craved alcohol. But my friend Robin supported me through this challenging time. She was my rock.

I felt as though I had lost everything once more. My husband had left me with all the bills, forcing me to learn how to pull myself out of it. I lost my best friend, the love of my life, a father figure, and my strength and desire to move forward all in one legal document.

I moved in with Robin and her husband, as they had offered me space and I had nowhere else to go. While

I greatly appreciated their kindness, I mourned my husband deeply. I entered a phase of bargaining, believing that if I improved myself, he would return. There I was, trying to "fix" things again. I had lost someone truly special and endured months of grief, attempting to restore our marriage, but to no avail. So much was lost, and nothing gained. But I still had one thing no one could take from me - my sobriety.

I was overrun with feelings of worthlessness and loss. Once again, I was overwhelmed.

Starting over was daunting. I began seeing the female counselor, and I was initially distrustful and suspicious of her. As we discussed my stepson's suicide, memories started to surface, memories of death and life that I struggled to make sense of.

I had two spirit guides from my youth; they served as my conscience, helping me make decisions and stay on track. It may seem odd or peculiar to others, but it was what I knew. The counselor, a Christian, assured me that God would care for me, embrace me, and offer a new life, rescuing me from danger. She explained that inviting Him into my heart would lead to forgiveness.

My heart was a frightening place, dark and detached, avoiding attachment to anything or anyone. I had learned that getting close to people usually ended with excruciating physical, mental and emotional injury. I began experiencing night terrors and feared I might harm myself during these episodes. Constantly contemplating suicide, I struggled to find the peace she described. I yearned for what she described although I had no idea where to even start searching for it. It was like being in the middle of the desert and finding a sign that said Food and Shelter – 5 miles. But the sign was lying on the ground, and I didn't know which direction it had originally pointed. This is the very definition of being "lost"

I confided in Robin, which heightened my fears of demons still residing within me. It was like they were obscured during the day only to emerge at night. That evening, she filled the bathtub with water and baptized me, believing it would help demons to come out. I didn't fully understand this, but I was frantic, and I had a willingness to try anything that might work. Robin saw me through some difficult places, but we also had some wild and fun times. I cherish all these memories.

Journaling

Who am I? Very hard question. I present as something I am not. I can act how I need to be looked at. I have needs deep down that I never will release because I don't trust anyone with that stuff. It is able to bring me to instant tears and is what makes me cry the most. It breaks my heart open and my heart cries a lot. I wanted to be a good daughter...

What is my purpose: To make people happy

What do I want: To feel my heart alive. To be able to really love someone. To see a red heart and not a black one.

Chapter 13

We are kept from the experience of Spirit because our inner world is cluttered with past traumas . . . As we begin to clear away this clutter, the energy of divine light and love begins to flow through our being.

Thomas Keating

My counselor also invited me to attend church, and I decided to go. Doing so put my loyalty and vows to my family at risk. I found myself caught between two worlds: one filled with terror, the other offering peace. During this period, I have little memory of specific events, as a fierce internal battle was raging for my soul. I stayed confused, caught in a whirlwind of visceral emotions, inner confusion and spiritual upheaval. I still felt unworthy of help and continued to trust no one. Robin and her husband relapsed, further undermining my stability. I wondered if I would ever find a safe place. Perhaps church could provide that safety. I chose to give it a try.

Journaling

I feel so wounded, so wounded. The scars still
seep, the wounds are old, very old but they
continue to seep. How do they heal, who can
rescue me, not Satan, Not God, has to be me. My
heart is black. How can I love me. Do I just
go up and hug the inner child, Charlotte? Will
that make the wounds stop seeping?

The church was a small-town country church, and I engaged in Sunday School and attended a Friday Bible Study. I began being teachable about the power and steadfastness of God. I found myself in church as often as I could. I was intrigued by the comfort I was starting to feel.

After Robin's relapse, I saw less of her. Her daughter had a baby whom I began helping to care for. Spending time with the baby made me feel valued and gave me a sense of purpose. He filled a significant void in my heart, giving me reason to live. I felt needed again.

I continued counseling, addressing issues about God, my spirit guides and how to "see" God working in my life. I moved into my own home and started working as a technician at a halfway house for adolescents. The woman that ran the house noticed my ability to help others and took an interest in me. I loved my life at this point; I was contributing to others' lives, feeling worthy, and becoming more open-minded about the concept of God. The baby and I regularly attended church, and during the week I met the needs of the adolescents. I could feel that seed of hope starting to grow and take root.

My counselor also began comparing my first marriage with my upbringing, which involved rituals, ceremonies, dressing in regalia, and worshiping a Great Spirit. That lifestyle was familiar and felt natural to me, aligning with my husband's beliefs. It all made sense, like a "moment of clarity". I began to realize that I felt quite comfortable in that experience and started to question whether it was the ritual setting rather than love that sustained me through the marriage. However, I genuinely felt a sense of peace and a connection to a Higher Power rooted in Indian culture. Over time, I transitioned from my Indian spirituality to a more abstract belief in a higher power I could feel but not see.

The promises made to me gradually appeared more evident. I immersed myself in church activities, attended Bible studies, and sought guidance from spiritual mentors, namely Roberta and Ginger. A special couple, Glen and Carrie, befriended me and consistently made me feel welcomed. They invested considerable time in my life and the life of the child I was helping raise. They served as role models and taught valuable life skills through their example. The people of God helped me understand that I had value and God valued my life. I was finally getting the spiritual guidance that I craved. The seed of hope had become a small plant, slowing breaking through the soil and emerging fresh and new.

I continued counseling and developed a close friendship with someone who was also connected to Joann, my counselor. She was very supportive during this period. I often discussed my counseling sessions with her, and she was unafraid to listen to my experiences. Memories began to surface which created more questions about my identity. I felt unworthy and self-disgusted, questioning whether I should have done something to escape my circumstances, despite being a child at the time. I was looking at my childhood and interpreting it with an adult mind. I was starting to gain the focus I never had as a child. When I reviewed where I had been I failed to appreciate where I had gotten to because my adult self was appalled by what I had found.

I shared many of these feelings with this friend, and she was very supportive. When I felt the call to trust in Jesus, my counselor was on vacation, so I called my friend. She led me to Jesus Christ that night, February 14, 1995. I was ten years sober, and she guided me through the sinner's prayer. I remember that day as if it were yesterday.

After I prayed, the then three-year-old baby walked across my bedroom and pulled out a VCR from a box. It was "The Greatest Story Ever Told," a Christian movie. I felt a sense of freedom and hope with this decision. My seed of hope was growing taller and started to produce leaves.

The following Sunday, I walked down the aisle at church, told my pastor I had accepted Christ, and expressed my desire to be baptized. As soon as I said those words, the lights in the church began flickering. The next week, during my baptism, a lightning strike caused a loud boom as I went underwater. I believe my spiritual ties were severed during this period. This event remains a significant memory for me, and both Glen and Carrie, who live near us today, confirm that this moment truly happened.

My friend started researching the religion I was raised in and became increasingly curious of it. She asked me questions about topics I was not yet ready to discuss. Eventually, she became deeply involved in acquiring knowledge about that religion and developed an interest in it. I felt betrayed, lost, and exploited. I wondered if I had influenced others beyond my upbringing. Around this time, my counselor told me she was moving out of state and would no longer be here to counsel me. I was devastated and retreated into myself. I continued to attend church and became very engrossed in my job and helping people. Helping others was one way I could always give my self a sense of worth when I was down.

I discovered my passion for my career and began training to become a Counselor in Training (CIT) specializing in Substance Abuse. During this time, I worked with a guy at the center for adolescents who showed interest in me. We had previously connected in Alcoholics Anonymous circles, and I was aware of him, but fear of rejection prevented me from pursuing anything. Working alongside him, I observed his genuine compassion for others, particularly the adolescents we served. We shared similar perspectives on helping others. His name is David.

We were working together, but we were also on a committee to put on the state convention for the Substance Abuse Counselors Organization in our state. He was the Chairman of the committee, and I was the Secretary. We had to print up some documents for committee business. This was before the days when everyone had a computer or a laptop at their fingertips. But I knew that my friend Robin had a computer we could use.

I met David at Robin's house, and we got a lot of work done. I found him easy to work with on these projects, and we joked and laughed throughout the process. I did not realize Robin was focused on how we interacted. After he left, she told me that David would be my next husband. I didn't give it a second thought, because I felt like I had failed in that area of my life, and I couldn't possibly find anyone who would be that interested in me.

One night I was working late at the halfway house and David was also still at work. I found out that I could go home earlier than I expected. When I mentioned getting off work early, he made a comment about maybe he could go to my house and watch a movie or something. I seized the opportunity and said that it would be okay. I was excited, nervous and frightened all at the same time.

All I had at the house was children's movies, so I asked him if he would bring a VCR movie when he came over. David had a young son, so his video collection was limited to Barney, the Teletubbies and similar movies. He found the movie Babe, and we agreed that it would be our evening entertainment.

Once he got to my house, we started the movie. We ended up lying on a palate of blankets on the floor.

We were cuddling while we watched the movie. I felt elated to not be alone. One thing led to another, and I ended the celibacy that started at the demise of my marriage.

We stayed up and talked about where we were in life. He had divorced about 2-3 years earlier and his son was about 4 years old. He had moved into his parents' house when he got divorced, and his son was with him and his parents most of the time. The child's mother had relapsed and was a very inconsistent character in his life. Her first name was the same as my first name. David also explained that his mother had become the primary caregiver for his son, because he worked full time.

I informed David that attending church would be a requirement if we pursue a relationship. He consented, and we began our relationship. He now tells people he would have gone anywhere with me.

David and I spent a lot of time together for the next month. The conference we were working on was just one month away, so we had plenty of reasons to get together. He also stayed overnight at my house several times. I opened up to him slowly about my past. I didn't want to get attached and then lose him if he found out about my history and didn't accept me.

David didn't criticize me and accepted what I told him. He also shared things with me about his life that he wasn't proud of, but I also accepted him and his past.

After achieving sobriety and beginning to confront my past, I became emotionally detached from my sexuality. The impact of past abuse has been significant and challenging to overcome. My upbringing and sense of self-worth were deeply shaped by issues related to sexuality and money. I sought validation from my mother through how I did with my sexual relationships.

Growing up, when the time came to have children, I chose not to pursue motherhood to avoid participating in the breeding process. During my first marriage, I did not use protection and did not conceive.

I now believe that upon accepting Christ and making spiritual changes, God restored that part of my body.

I relocated closer to my workplace and continued attending church. The child's parents assumed more responsibility for their son, allowing me to concentrate on my relationship with David and my academic pursuits. I did not seek counseling and instead based my self-esteem on my ability to help others. Over time, I noticed physical changes and, through testing, discovered I was pregnant. Although I initially thought it was a mistake, I was pregnant at 37 and felt a sense of joy. David and I shared a room during the conference, and I told him about my pregnancy on the first night we were there. David shared my excitement and said that we should get married. I agreed. In a month's time I had gone from being single with no real aspirations for a relationship to being pregnant and engaged! That plant of hope had grown tall and was starting to bud.

I felt quite nervous about informing my spiritual mentors, as I believed I had acted prematurely and was uncertain about their feelings towards my decision. I was such a harsh critic of myself and I always suspected others were judging me even worse. Fortunately, they were very supportive, offering grace and accepting my pregnancy. They also mentioned that I might have put the cart before the horse, but I was willing to accept that. Gaining validation from the people in my life was very important to me.

Our wedding was a modest ceremony attended by our pastor, a few witnesses, some of David's family, and my spiritual mentors. The ceremony was held in the confines of our Pastor's office. Roberta generously hosted our reception at her home. The event was joyful, and I experienced a profound sense of happiness in joining David's family.

During this period, David had to make a significant decision that affected David's family, and I became involved in the process. We sought counsel from Roberta and her husband, who was a retired judge. We prayed. We argued. We went through some really tough days.

Reflecting on my past and my desire for my mother's acceptance, David and I made a choice that was not entirely beneficial. We did not come to the decision easily or lightly, but we had to make a choice. With this choice we were re-locating about 4 hours away from his family.

I believe this decision affected my relationship with David's family and was influenced partially by my trauma and the importance I placed on attachment. I was genuinely excited about becoming part of a "Brady Bunch" family but quickly realized that there was hurt and dysfunction within this family as well. The stressors in his family were not immediately evident to me. My idea of family stress was quite different.

This situation remains a lingering question in my mind and has created a divide between me and my children, as well as a sense of not being fully accepted by his family. However, we are closer today; I love his family and would do anything for them.

As I mentioned, my husband received a job offer in a different city, prompting us to move away from our familiar surroundings. During this period, I discovered I was pregnant again, and we welcomed a baby girl. I took all the necessary precautions, similar to those I had with my first child.

After relocating, we found a church community where we quickly integrated. We were actively helping others, taking on various roles, and eventually leading a support group for individuals in and out of recovery. This involvement provided me with renewed purpose and meaning. My sense of self-worth was primarily based on serving others. We had an inspiring pastor who explained the Bible in a way I had never encountered before. I started to connect more deeply with fellow Christians, experiencing a growing sense of hope and peace. I drew inspiration from the spirituality of others to develop my own understanding, although I still felt I lacked a personal relationship with God; instead, my connection was mediated through people.

After a few years, our Pastor departed, and the church was in a state of flux that it never really recovered from. Around this time, just a few short years after my salvation and baptism, I experienced a period of emotional turmoil.

It came on slowly like an illness in my soul, getting a little stronger each day. Suddenly, I realized that I was feeling intense anger toward God. I believed I had been deprived of the opportunity to reconcile with my family because of my faith. There was no trial period to decide whether I wanted to continue living a saved life or revert to my previous beliefs. I had chosen Him over them and there was no customer service to help me if I decided to bring it back and exchange it; no refunds allowed.

Resolving these feelings and rebuilding my relationship with God took considerable time. It also created turmoil that strained against the callouses of my old wounds. On the surface, my connection with Him appeared strong, yet internally, I struggled between my new world and the loyalty I felt toward my family. They would now never meet the baby they had tried to take from me or witness my achievements. I still carried the emptiness that evolved from not feeling "good enough" for my mother's love.

I sought acceptance within the church, often using my past pain and trauma to fulfill my current emotional needs. I valued others' opinions of me and endeavored to care for everyone around me to feel worthy. I mimicked the behaviors I observed in others during worship, attempting to project an image of spiritual stability. I longed for the peace and serenity I saw other people wearing, but inside all I could see were my filthy rags.

Journaling

What's at the bottom of this hole. I have
searched for years to fill it with something
until today. My mom is at the bottom of this
hole and I put so much of myself in this hole,
never to be grounded but to always fade away to
nothingness. The spirit sits right above the
bottom keeping that hole from ever reaching out
and grabbing me. I search for my own. I stay
in a mess. I had to fill that hole with horror.
I thought I could please my mom, maybe this, do
I really need to feel my mom's acceptance after
so many years? I feel like a lost soul looking
for somewhere to blossom, but I can't find
where to land. I land in what's familiar, only
to feel the pain again and again and again.

I'm tired of landing here. Doesn't my soul
need to be attached somewhere? And I am looking
for something I am not going to find. My soul
wants to rest, but where? I know what I need but
where does it come from? Does it come from deep
within? Is there space for my new soul? What if
my happy comes back? Will they steal it away
again? I am tapping into a deep sense of being a
disappointment. I know my soul I was born with
was a happy soul, please come back. I want more
than ever for this spirit to leave me. My mom
is dead. She has nothing to offer me. She is
incapable of meeting any need of mine. We do

not have co-existing spirits. I want to have my
own spirit I was born with, not what was molded
and developed in me. I try so hard to pull from
within, happy memories, my babies, vacations,
and all that pulls up is pain. Please give me
back my born soul, please don't rob me anymore,
of who I was when I came out of my mother's
womb. Show me who I was before the new soul was
developed in me. This is not who I was meant to
be. Please release me spirit.

Chapter 14

*"Stop looking at today through yesterday's lens. Adjust
your focus and capture life in living color."*
                                                    Sanjo Jendayi

My body was filled with memories and trauma, yet I
lacked a way to process these feelings mentally. My
mind was a prison that restrained me from feeling
worthy, accepted and valued. I worshiped an invisible
God, who, based on sermons I listened to, was often
portrayed as mean, warlike, and angry creating
conflicts and killing children.

Despite this, I trusted that He could help me. The
Bible did not make sense to me because of the
teachings I got as a child. I kept confusing the old
Bible with the new one. But I knew I was different.
My plant inside me was surviving through a spiritual
winter.

My life remained busy, navigating through jobs that
tested my husband's integrity, and dedicating
ourselves to church activities and service. I completed
my counseling education and successfully passed both
the oral and written licensing exams, but... (there
always seems to be a "but" when things are going well)

– but I initially failed the written exam. This left me feeling disappointed. The oral exam involved presenting a case plan before four evaluators, which made me nervous, especially speaking in front of others. Despite this, I persevered and scored 99% on the oral exam. After retaking the written test, I earned my license as an Addiction Counselor. I felt pride in my accomplishment and my husband shared in my excitement. I had gone from the couch to the chair in the counseling office – full circle!

As our lives progressed, I became increasingly suspicious. I received information from a trusted source indicating that my family had resumed their search for me. To avoid contact, I decided to open a P.O. Box, believing that if they had a way to reach me some way, they would not attempt to find me, as my sister had previously. I communicated this to my source and soon began receiving various items, letters, ritual objects, medallions, and other artifacts trying to drag me back into their world of evil and chaos. My husband would often check the box and discard its contents before I saw them. I maintained the P.O. Box for approximately ten years, during which they never resumed their search for me.

My body was constantly in a state of fear, and memories of past trauma began resurfacing. I was not in counseling because I recognized that my issues were deeper than what previous therapy had addressed. I sought support from friends in the church, but they were unable to respond to my needs due to the sensitive nature of my trauma. The church seemed unwilling or unable to acknowledge or discuss the underlying issues.

So, I maintained a facade of happiness, helping others while I was suffering internally. My trauma repeatedly surfaced, leaving me with no safe space to process it. I started experiencing night terrors, during which my husband would find me in the attic reliving traumatic events or attempting self-harm. He would pray over me, asking for the Blood of Jesus to protect and heal me.

One morning after I woke up, David told me that I had a particularly bad night terror. He woke up to the sound of me banging my head against the footboard of the bed. He said that when he tried to stop me, I turned and spoke with a chilling deep voice that was not my own. He again prayed the blood of Jesus over me and told whatever was controlling me that I belonged to Jesus now, and it had to leave.

Thankfully, that episode was a one-time occurrence.

My husband became my safe person; he listened to my tears and my recounting of past events. His support helped me begin to trust again, and I realized that for the first time in my life, I was trusting someone without fear of being hurt.

My children were growing up, and I made sure they attended church regularly. They participated in every church event for children. Determined to break the cycle of generational curses I had learned about from the Bible, I was making sure they learned something different – better – than what I had experienced. Their "normal" was not the normal my family had thrust upon me.

As the staff changed at our church, we transitioned to a different congregation. Remember Glen and Carrie, whom I mentioned earlier? We visited a new church where Glen was on the staff. They had relocated to our city, and it was a joy to see them again. Eventually, we joined this church, with my children's approval, and started forming new friendships. It was comforting to have Glen and Carrie there, reminiscing about my salvation experience at our first church. I began to realize that I missed having memories of good times as a child and started reflecting on my identity. People often spoke about their families, holidays, parents, and childhood memories.

I started focusing on my identity, hearing that it belonged in Christ. This was another perplexing notion which I found myself wrestling. If that was true, then why did He give me an identity rooted in an imperfect family? I recalled my blue eyes - the only one among thirteen siblings to have them. Knowing I was different from my family at age six, I questioned where my true identity lay. Was it in my roots, my role as a mother and wife, or in Christ? I began to struggle with these questions, piecing together my understanding of myself.

One of the biggest challenges for me during this time was celebrating holidays and birthdays with my children. Having been brought up without these, I wanted the best for my children. Granted, my children have grown up and I feel assured they will do a better job when I have grandchildren, but I struggled in that area. People would say, just put up a tree, or just have a party for them. For me it went much deeper than that. I had no clue what I was actually celebrating. When you are raised in believing one thing for 22 years, it was very hard to begin seeing it as a happy time.

My son helped me stay focused in a way. The city we are in is known for putting up lights and decorations for Halloween. That was one of the highest "holy" days with my family, and I dreaded it every year. Anyway, my son would look for the Christmas lights that were going up after the Halloween lights came down. He started calling out "Jesus Lights!" when we drove past a display. Those simple two words brought relief and comfort to my soul.

While contemplating birthdays, I realized I was responding to myself and my unworthiness to even have children and the fun and excitement that children gave me. It all was carrying back to my own unworthiness. This is very difficult to explain, and I may never have words to explain it, but holidays reinforced my unworthiness. They reminded me that I was different. Somehow, I was missing something I never had.

The pastor's wife, who was also a counselor, became a resource for me as I sought to understand myself and my place in the world. After more than ten years without counseling, I decided to try again. Our sessions focused on my identity in Christ Jesus, exploring scripture, and how I was created in His image. I was reminded that I am a precious child of

God, loved unconditionally. Despite this, questions lingered in my mind: Why? Why does God let the rain fall on the parched plant?

I questioned how I perceived God whether as a loving deity or as a figure of hate and sacrifice. I wondered about the God who seemed to see me as unworthy of life beyond my birth circumstances, and about the pain inflicted by my mother. I had always felt a distant intimacy with her. She was close, by far out of my reach at the same time. She would not, or could not, provide a safe environment.

I wrestled silently with many of these questions. My counselor helped me to see God's character more clearly, providing guidance and understanding. Growing under her guidance, I engaged in Bible studies, assumed roles within the church, and ensured my children were engaged in the youth group. She was instrumental in my spiritual development, helping me deepen my Christian knowledge. Through her support, I was confident in my acceptance of Jesus as my Savior. I believe in his death, crucifixion, and resurrection. However, my faith was still challenged by doubts about his actions and his invisibility. I continued to seek validation from the people around me, finding worth and acceptance in their presence. An internal cry for fulfillment persisted within me.

Chapter 15

My church announced a mission trip to Haiti, which sparked my interest. Recognizing that Haiti is a developing country facing spiritual challenges, I was drawn to participate in a ministry focused on aiding children with special needs. This organization provides care for children who are abandoned or left on porches, seeking families to adopt and nurture them.

I was very enthusiastic about the trip.

During a layover in a city significant to my past, there were problems with airline scheduling which evolved into an unexpectedly stay overnight. After settling in a hotel, we went sightseeing, visiting a place filled with memories from my past. My companions encouraged me to confront my fears, promising support. As I approached my fears, a rainbow appeared in the distance, which I interpret as a sign from God affirming my worth and reassurance that everything is okay. This was one of the first times I recognized how much things of nature are tied into my understanding of God and how He shows me things through His creation.

Upon arriving in Port-au-Prince, Haiti, we drove several hours to our destination. Throughout the journey, I sensed a spiritual darkness that seemed to align with the country's predominant religion, Voodoo. As we familiarized ourselves with the area and interacted with local villagers, this pervasive sense of darkness became increasingly evident, helping me understand why I was here. I understood the feeling of the darkness; I was raised in it.

During our time in Haiti, I was asked to share my testimony with a group of young adult Haitians. I had never presented my testimony publicly before. I wasn't nearly as detailed as I've been here because I had not overcome so much of my past yet. But this was a new phase of using my personal history for the glory of the Creator.

I was quite nervous. An interpreter translated my words for the people. As I spoke, I was hearing my life events put into words from beginning to end for the first time. Honestly, I don't remember exactly which of the horrors I recounted that day. It was evident to me that what I was sharing was something relatable for many in the group. I didn't have to understand what the interpreter was saying to feel the impact on my audience. I could also sense the unease of some of the group as they appeared to see themselves in the mirror I had become.

In conclusion, I shared about the rainbow I saw on the way to their country. I spoke about my salvation in Christ.

As I finished, the people began pointing upward: there was another rainbow in the sky! It felt as if God was sending me a message of belonging amongst these people. Many young adults shared with me their struggles with spiritual warfare in Haiti.

While taking a walking tour of the village, I noticed many elderly individuals slept outside their homes, either on porches or on the ground. Conversations revealed that their children practiced Voodoo, and the elders avoided sleeping indoors due to spirits believed to inhabit their homes.

Accompanied by Andrea from the ministry "My Life Speaks", I walked through the village, praying for spiritual healing and wholeness for the villagers. We often paused to pray for individuals battling spiritual warfare. I believe that God revealed my purpose through this experience, and I was allowed to use my past trauma to assist others facing similar struggles.

I developed a deep appreciation for Haiti and the significance it brought to my life. I felt a sense of purpose in understanding spiritual warfare. And this time I was on the right side of the battle! My existence was significant to the people around me. God was showing me my true value in His Kingdom. The children we served were precious, and the ministry provided daily lunches for over 200 kids, offering them love and care while providing for a basic, practical need.

I left a piece of my heart in Haiti. I was able to return to that country four times. A second ministry we worked with, LA Reach Haiti, ministered in a different way. They built housing for children who were economic orphans and thereby created stability for their parents and reunification for their families. We also were able to help build wells, providing a safe source of clean water for the communities. I had the opportunity to walk around the ministry's property and undo ceremonial circles made of rock that had been created there for clandestine rituals and ceremonies.

Unfortunately, the evil and corruption that runs rampant in Haiti has led to great unrest. I have been unable to return to the country that holds my heart. I frequently pray for the people of Haiti and for the spiritual darkness that has plunged the nation into chaos to be overcome by the Light of the World.

Each time I returned to the United States, I was reminded of how God has used aspects of my past to assist those we served in Haiti.

I hope to rejoin the supernatural struggle not just in my heart, but in person again someday. It disappoints and disgusts me that such a beautiful country has been swallowed up by so much evil. I continue to pray for a relief of the ethereal death grip will be lifted and the streets will become safe for our trips to resume. I was starting to fully grasp the value that my story had in comforting, restoring, and encouraging others.

At 16, I witnessed my friend's tragic death when he was shot and killed by my brother. I never imagined that God could use my horrifying experience to help someone else.

My husband and I became active in our church's youth ministry, and each summer, we served as counselors at the church youth camp. We would take off on a 4-day weekend trip to drive several hours to a camp in the middle of Nowhere, Texas. We appreciated the activities and sense of community there. I had learned personally that escaping from my day-to-day environment often gave me opportunity to refocus my mind on things of eternal importance. I saw this happening with the youth of our church and was proud to be part of it.

One evening, after a service at camp, a girl approached me seeking counseling. She was deeply upset over a recent tragedy. Her boyfriend was shot and killed in a drive-by shooting while they were in her vehicle. During our conversations about good and evil and the senselessness of his death, I realized that God was using this unresolved trauma to help her. My experience enabled me to connect with her and reassure her that she was not alone in her grief. I saw another circle closing: I was the person I so intensely craved when no one was there for me.

My faith in God was growing as I began to see Him working in my life. I was engaged in the Bible and had a hunger to study with other ladies in my church. My husband and I had opened a private practice for Substance Abuse clients many years back and I was able to use some of my experiences in guiding others spiritually. If God was there after all I had been through and done, I could proclaim that He is there for them. The hope that was sowed in my heart became one of many plants in a garden.

I was finally beginning to make Him Lord over my life, but I was missing the inner peace I sought. As previously mentioned, my husband and I aimed to create a safe and welcoming environment in our home. Since our marriage, we have hosted several dozen individuals and families without expecting anything in return. We have found joy in serving others and witnessing their recovery, restoration, and progress.

They have diverse situations that put them in need of a safe place, ranging from getting out of dangerous life circumstances, being homeless due to a hurricane, and moving into town for a job and not having a place yet. They have been friends, neighbors, church members, co-workers, family of friends and occasionally strangers.

Chapter 16

"There are wounds that never show on the body that are deeper and more hurtful than anything that bleeds."
Laurell K. Hamilton

Remember my friend Robin? She was a recurring presence in our lives, often reminiscing about our past endeavors during her sober periods. She moved in with us at one point; yet another full circle from when I moved in with her. A particularly severe relapse into addiction forced us to ask her to leave. Robin lived in various places before returning to an abusive husband seeking refuge. Early one morning, her husband called to inform me that Robin had taken her own life the night before. Horrified and shocked, I could not believe that she had done such a thing. Not that she hadn't talked about it before. She even went to the hospital once or twice with similar idections. But this was different. This was real.

Her husband said he and his ex-wife had already cleaned her body before the police arrived. I was left to inform her daughter and family about her death.

My denial was so strong, but I couldn't wake up from the nightmare of losing her.

Overwhelmed with grief, guilt, shame, and a sense of despair, I felt as though I was losing hope. Despite my 30 years of sobriety, I was overwhelmed by the desire to drink. Yet I was unable to imagine how someone could relapse after such a long time sober, like she did. Although I resisted the temptation to drink, I gained a deeper appreciation for the fragility of sobriety and the pain that can trigger relapse. Robin's memory remains vivid in my mind, and I will always value the profound influence she had on my life.

The bond we shared was beyond friendship. She was a survivor, as was I. We were, and still are, connected at the soul. I still think about her and talk about her often. The memories of her reinforce that I can have fun even in some of the most trying situations. I still have her driver's license tucked away in a special place.

A strong oak that stood by my plant of hope had been taken away by a drought. I can no longer bask in her shade when the days get hot.

Chapter 17

> *"Healing from trauma can also mean strength and joy. The goal of healing is not a papering-over of changes in an effort to preserve or present things as normal. It is to acknowledge and wear your new life – warts, wisdom, and all – with courage."*
>
> Catherine Woodiwiss

My children grew into adulthood. Seeing them grow up and find their own way was exciting and scary. I was assured that they would be okay because of their spiritual upbringing and the fact that they had parental help, which I so sorely lacked at that time of my life. They also had friends they could rely on. My husband and I had done what we could to give them a firm foundation.

My son surrendered to his call to the ministry when he was a senior in High School. Following that call, he attended a Christian College in the state we live in. He excelled in Biblical languages and started teaching himself Hebrew while he was taking Greek. When he graduated from his undergraduate program, he went straight into a master's program. He completed a degree in Biblical Languages. He is now an associate pastor at the church I attend. Not only has he broken the generational curse, but he has gone full circle and turned the curse upside down.

My daughter struggled with significant medical issues as she grew up. She is a real champ, and she worked so hard to find ways to triumph over her obstacles rather than let them defeat her. As she grew up we got her involved with horses because of both the physical benefits in developing her muscles and the therapeutic value of caring for horses. She has become quite the equestrian and has won her share of blue ribbons in competition. She is currently working at a veterinarian clinic and thrives on caring for the animals.

About the time the kids were leaving the house, my husband and I formed a bond with a pregnant woman battling addiction. We met her through a friend from church who was also battling addiction. He was in a treatment program and one of the other people there had told him about his girlfriend, who was pregnant. She was supporting her habit by using what she had to satisfy people that had what she needed. He asked us to get in touch with her and her family to try and find some help.

I contacted her and her family, and we formulated a plan. She just happened to be in the state where I was born, but there was no way she could get clean and stay clean in that environment. I drove half-way to where she lived, and her mother brought her half-way so we could meet in the middle. We arrived at Walmart parking lot, she left her mom's car and jumped in mine, and off we went.

I assisted her in accessing treatment and supported her recovery journey. When her baby was born, he had to go through detox in the hospital. She stayed with the baby for 4 weeks as he grew stronger. Once he was released, he stayed with us. She went into a sober living program due to her ongoing struggles. She did well for a while, then she would struggle again. Addiction has a way of taking over a person's life and it does not want to turn loose.

After about 3 years we adopted her son at her request. He has had struggles of his own, and we have been right there with him throughout. Now nine years old, he is a source of joy in our lives. His mother fell victim to the fentanyl crisis and passed after overdosing 3 years later. This has profoundly affected us. Despite his autism, he remains a gentle and loving child

Despite outward efforts to find fulfillment, I felt a lingering internal emptiness. The only hope I clung to was filling my sense of unworthiness with relationships. My husband and I discussed becoming foster parents, and he agreed. We completed the certification process and started caring for foster children. Many asked if it was difficult to give the children back, but we believed that providing a stable, loving environment for six months to a year would give them a solid foundation. We encouraged their reunification with their families by supporting the bio parents in seeking help and maintaining strong relationships. Over four years, we fostered more than forty children, witnessing many reunions and incredible growth in children and families.

As evident now, I often reverted to familiar patterns, primarily basing my self-worth on my ability to serve others. This tendency originated early in life and kept me anchored in past experiences.

Around this time, I was invited to a spiritual retreat, Discovery Weekend. It took me a year to summon the courage to attend. It was supposed to be a weekend "retreat" to help build your relationship with God.

When the time arrived, I felt extremely nervous. Attending alone, my focus was entirely on myself, and I was seeking something, though I wasn't quite sure what. Pushing my apprehensions aside, I tried to keep an open mind. This was outside of my comfort zone, as they say. This was WAY outside of my comfort zone. The retreat's motto is "36 hours could change your life," and indeed, it renovated mine.

My nameplate read – Rebecca, Daughter of the King – and the reverse side displayed a quote, "What if I fall? Oh, but darling, what if you fly!" I longed to soar, to find happiness and joy, yet I continued to carry the weight of my past identity, filled with shame and guilt.

Throughout the weekend, I experienced a profound sense of freedom. There were no rules or obligations associated with being spiritual. I connected with myself and, through nature, was able to sit alone in silence. My mind was free from the barrage of old messages, and I felt an unprecedented inner peace. I was free from judgment regarding my past actions.

My mental processes were unburdened. There were no religious rules I felt compelled to follow to be considered good; it was simply about being spiritual in my own way. I finally understood what they meant by "having a personal relationship with God". My commitment to Christ remained steadfast; this retreat demonstrated that I could express my relationship with Him in diverse ways, which He would provide.

I left the retreat feeling uplifted and eager for more of that peace. I had a better understanding of my direct relationship with my Creator. I learned I didn't have to follow man's rules to have a relationship with the Architect of the Universe.

I came off that weekend with new direction and yearning to maintain that same peace in my head. I began looking at church much differently, realizing I was following a lot of rules and commands, much like the religion I was raised in. A very slow light began forming in my spirit. I began comparing what Spirituality felt like with the absence of man-made rules.

Journaling

I am a very strong person that needs to believe that. Being rescued. Someone rescue me. Pieces are going together. I have no identity but now many identities.

Those stairs, white To many feelings, Brillo pads, bleach. Purpose in life. I think I have great purpose. I just can' t find it. How do you go into a brain for purpose or memory and can' t find it.

I would love to be rescued. I wonder how it would be if I had been rescued? If someone cared enough to rescue me to put their life on the line to save me. Maybe I would be different. Maybe I would have become worthy. If they would have come to find me Oh never mind. My family was not looking for me, they were doing it.

I wish I could just be a child and someone just rescue me.

Our church's pastor retired, and my counseling sessions concluded, marking the end of a significant chapter in my spiritual and personal journey. As new staff members joined, we became increasingly skeptical about the church's direction, perceiving a shift towards prioritizing current members over outreach efforts. There was also a perceived shift toward legalism following "the rules".

This led to conflict between my husband and I and the new pastor, resulting in our decision to part ways with the church. We also stepped away from a recovery program we had initiated there.

I began to realize that imperfections exist within the church community; that all men are sinful. No one is perfect. My old spiritual faith became fragile, especially since I had tied my self-worth to the opinions of others. I experienced a deep fall, losing trust in people. My children, now young adults, were pursuing their paths. My son in ministry and my daughter excelling in horse shows and breaking racehorses.

I regarded church members as my family and sought to fulfill my need for connection through their support. Over time, some members criticized our efforts to assist broken and homeless individuals who had little to offer in return. Conversely, others provided encouragement and volunteered to serve as mentors for those less fortunate.

In our church, the criteria for baptism were established through human decision-making processes in business meetings with people deciding if these people were saved appropriately. Recognizing the emotional toll and the internal conflicts arising from these experiences, we decided to pause our church activities to focus on healing from the emotional wounds inflicted within our own family. This period of reflection and recovery was essential to regain strength and clarity before resuming our community service efforts.

We experienced a profound loss, everyone gone in a single day. I sank into myself, questioning what I was doing wrong. I had dedicated my energy to serving the church, helping the homeless, supporting trauma-affected children, working with my clients, and caring for my family. Yet, I wondered if I was doing enough or if I had made mistakes.

I had tasted something different, and I wanted that peace I felt at Discovery. But the enemy is quick to attack and destabilize any spiritual growth. My precious tree of hope had grown tall, and someone came along and broke it off at the trunk.

Chapter 18

> *"Someone who has experienced trauma also has gifts to offer all of us - in their depth, their knowledge of our universal vulnerability, and their experience of the power of compassion."*
>
> *Sharon Salzberg*

I had experienced recurring trauma and felt uncertain about my future steps. I sought assistance from various counselors, exploring techniques such as brain spotting and EMDR, but struggled to establish meaningful connections and ultimately ceased seeking help. When I surrender, I tend to revert to familiar patterns. My search for self-worth was challenging; I believed I was unworthy of others' time and hesitant to burden anyone with my needs.

I had a foster teenager who confided in me about her involvement in occult practices and her conflicts with attending church. She was also distressed by her friends' participation in animal abuse. We arranged for her to see a therapist, who appeared knowledgeable in these areas and accepted her as a client. However, my foster daughter was reluctant to discuss these issues and began to act out. Ultimately, she was placed in a long-term children's home that specialized in addressing children with behavioral challenges.

I continued to struggle to identify what was truly happening within me. Despite fulfilling all expectations attending church services both morning and evening, volunteering for Vacation Bible School, serving as a camp counselor, co-facilitating a recovery group, and undertaking various other responsibilities I again felt disconnected from God's presence in my heart. I was actively fostering children, raising my adopted son, and providing counseling through my practice, all while ensuring my family's needs were met. Yet, I couldn't understand why I didn't feel God's presence again. I just couldn't do enough to feel his daily presence in my life.

I sought medical advice, adjusted medications, confessed my sins, and took responsibility for my mistakes, (even those I believed were not mine to carry). When I felt like a burden or experienced feelings of rejection, I would withdraw from situations. The cycle continued, leaving me searching for spiritual fulfillment and understanding.

I desired those moments of inner peace at the Discovery Weekend, a desire to "fly," and have a feeling of worthiness while alone in God's creation. I yearned to recapture that feeling. However, I questioned how to find it within the boundaries of religion. Remembering the therapist my foster child had seen, I felt a desire to reconnect with her to work on finding that peace again.

Noel accepted me as a client and reassured me that hope was possible. I explained my feelings of being trapped in my religious upbringing, re-living childhood experiences in adulthood, and seeking acceptance by striving to be the best for my mother and others. I knew the cycle, but I had not found the key to unlock its grip on me.

It took several months to establish trust. I desired a therapist who could address trauma from a psychological perspective. I was confident in my relationship with God, and my therapist assured me that this did not need to change. Conversely, she encouraged me to explore different healing methods for trauma.

Gradually, I shared parts of my past, often fearing I would break the loyalty vow I made as a child. It felt liberating to release these memories, but I also sensed a deep internal unrest. As I processed some traumatic events, I visualized a baby screaming in terror, reliving those moments.

My therapist introduced the concept of an inner child, which helped explain the inner voice I was experiencing. She began to clarify how the brain processes complex trauma. Complex trauma results from repeated exposure to trauma – especially when there appears no way to escape. Initially, I was apprehensive about this explanation, fearing I might resemble my mother, who had multiple personalities.

However, I realized that my experience was different. My brain had to compartmentalize my trauma because it couldn't process everything at once. I started re-processing the experiences that my mind could not or would not process when they happened.

The emotional releases facilitated by this process enabled my child to experience feelings she had suppressed for many years. She would cry extensively, ultimately finding an outlet for her emotions. The protectors would intervene to ensure her safety, and I would reassure them that she was now secure enough to begin healing. My inner child was starting to rely on me for protection. I was both exhilarating and incredibly vulnerable.

Journaling

It didn't work again and again leaving me feeling of no use again. I felt like I did good in the beginning. I was trained. I want to ask about an apparatus, the kind I learned on simple hook from ceiling, spring, rope and seat with opening. Simple. They have total control of me and up and down, turning me different ways. My mind wants to twist off. I understand through my therapy I need to create enough energy in myself to pull me through this thinking and I can't. Well, I have survived and will continue to.

Approximately a year into therapy, I participated in a retreat called Tapping into Wellness. This event piqued my interest, especially after attending a Discovery Weekend. The retreat lasted four days and featured activities such as nature hikes, intuitive readings, yoga, and forest bathing and massages. I chose to attend alone, like my decision for the Discovery Weekend, aiming to focus on myself and initiate healing from within.

My inner child was deeply wounded, and with no distractions, I sought to concentrate on her and provide her with some respite from the negative messages I had been feeding her. I enjoyed getting my feet dirty on the nature trails, exploring various plants, and collecting items to create a collage later. This retreat marked the first time I felt a genuine connection with my inner child. I now had a visual image of her, which allowed me to begin giving her an identity, a clearer understanding of who she was and to start the healing process.

Journaling

I allowed baby to come close to my heart today. Was it actually her coming to me or me coming to her, or did we meet in the middle. I am not sure, maybe we ran into each other. I floated around the heart not sure of how to go in, or if I'm even ready. My baby met Rebecca only for a flit of a second. I felt naked and exposed, vulnerable and full of fear. I began exploring my, what was that, what the f--k was that. Back down I go escaping the fast fear out in the open, exposed. Back to safety. I felt pressure, pressure, scared, not scared, scared, pressure. Were they coming to get me, waiting, waiting, pressure again. Light, no hurt, no hurt yet, yet my body feels in flames. Soft, no hurt, touching my flesh, no hurt, no hurt, soft. What do I do, where do I go. Sensation makes me feel warm. OK it's gone, but it didn't hurt me, smooth, constantly baby scared. What

was it. Not as scared, safe, back in my safe
space

Chapter 19

I continued my therapy journey, gaining clarity on my personal growth path. I created a secure space for my inner child, protecting her from harm when I was outside safe environments. This process allowed me to confront the wounds inflicted by my mother, including distressing images that kept me in a state of freeze. I also began forming connections with like-minded individuals. Despite numerous moments of temptation to give up or revert to old patterns, I persisted in my healing process. I started to trust my therapist as she helped me recognize my worth and helped me understand that I was not responsible for the events that occurred. She reassured me that making decisions as a child, often with adult responsibilities, was complex and that there were no clear right answers when facing consequences.

Regardless of my choices, I experienced pain, which was an inevitable part of my growth process.

 # Journaling

Looking at my little girl, tears justify behaviors, or they blame myself. Vows, loyalty to family, really deep pain, fear, anxiety, not good enough, death, emotional trauma, identifying the pain. Leave it alone, my space where the universe put me, understanding the pain my child went through now as an adult.

Consequence

Throughout my therapy, my husband has been a consistent source of support and stability. He has shown remarkable patience and understanding. My children have been my biggest supporters, celebrating my progress. My children have broken the cycle of generational challenges, and I am proud to be their mother. My 9-year-old son continues to face challenges with autism due to his addiction at birth but is making significant strides in understanding his emotions.

Connecting with my inner child at each stage of development involved recognizing their perceptions and understanding that they were not at fault. I sought permission from my protectors, who were designed to ensure my safety. During this process, I experienced anger, a challenging emotion for me, as I had learned to associate sadness with safety during my upbringing. With the support of my therapist, I gained a better understanding of anger, which facilitated a deeper connection with my inner self. I realized that I had previously blamed them for what happened to me.

My participation in retreats has facilitated personal growth, providing a distraction-free environment that allows for self-reflection. These experiences have helped me to understand and cope with grief, including the loss of my idealized family, which I was unable to create. During one retreat, I created a memorial for my sacrificed baby and released her spirit in a serene lake surrounded by cypress trees. Taking time away from responsibilities I imposed on myself has helped me to feel deserving, to absorb the healing power of nature, and to gain valuable insights.

I have experienced significant growth in my spirituality, which has gained new significance for me. I have moved beyond religion, which was often defined by the rules and rituals of a church, and now draw strength from nature. While I value my church community for the friendships and support it provides, I realized I was equating my worth with what I could contribute, which hindered my connection with God.

Through reflection, especially recalling my first sense of connection during Discovery Weekend, I understood that God's Word offers much more to me. I have a solid belief in God now and He has given me a path to follow.

I believe that He knows each one of us and that we all have sinful natures. None but He will provide me with what I need and desire. He knows my past and I truly believe He spared my mental health growing up.

He has given me a deep perspective on nature and has made it a connection to Him for me. When experiencing feelings of struggle, depression, or happiness, I find solace in nature, where I can sense His magnificent power.

Nature, for me, embodies a range of beliefs and practices that foster a spiritual connection with the natural world. It highlights the interconnections of all living beings, and I often consider nature as sacred or spiritually significant. I am able to experience awe and wonder in the natural environment and engaging in practices such as mindfulness in nature and creating healing inspired by natural elements.

I am currently in the process of personal growth, having previously based my self-worth on others' acceptance. Rejection often leaves me feeling lost and affected deeply. I am working through therapy, specifically EMDR, which helps me recover from trauma and distressing life experiences. This therapy involves recalling disturbing memories while engaging in bilateral stimulation, such as eye movements, which is believed to lessen the emotional impact of these memories. My goal is to foster a sense of self-worth and recognize that I am deserving of self-care and nurturing in all aspects of my being.

Chapter 20

I recently attended a retreat in Costa Rica, a country renowned for its natural beauty and safety. During this experience, I engaged in various healing activities, including intuitive readings, sound baths, Reiki, and pool yoga, which fostered a sense of peace and self-care. The environment was vibrant with wildlife, featuring monkeys in the trees and wild sloths where I had the opportunity to feed and pet. This immersion in nature fostered a sense of freedom that resonated deeply with my inner child, making her feel safe and open. As a result, she became more receptive to exploring her trauma, leading to the realization that I had been living a lie by defending my mother and accepting blame for the trauma inflicted upon me. I recognized my protective instincts towards her. In Costa Rica, I found the ideal environment to begin this exploration. I enjoyed the steadfast support of a trusted group of attendees with whom I had built rapport through previous retreats. I was able to speak openly about my mother, my soulmate, and my siblings, without assigning blame to myself.

Experiencing this freedom allowed me to properly address and process the trauma and pain. Expressing my voice for the first time outside a counseling session regarding past experiences with my inner child was a significant milestone. It was liberating to articulate what had been done to me and how it influenced my adult life.

One of the key insights I gained from the retreat was to ask myself, "Does this add value to my life?" This question has helped me close chapters related to actions I took in pursuit of self-worth. I now evaluate each situation through this lens and remain committed to actions that enhance my self-energy and self-worth.

On the final day of the retreat, I realized I could not find my passport. After searching everywhere, we went to the airport, but it was not there, nor had it been turned in to the embassy. When I understood I would not be able to fly back with my group, a wave of fear overwhelmed me. I felt uncertain about how to handle the situation. Alone in a foreign country, aware that my group had responsibilities awaiting them at home, I did not feel worthy enough for anyone to waste time on me. I had accepted my consequences for my lack of responsibility.

While pondering my situation, a friend stepped in to support me. Her presence provided a sense of safety, knowing I would not be alone. She knew how to use Uber, a service I had never used before, and found us a hostel, which was unfamiliar to me. We contacted the embassy, but it was closed until Monday. I wanted to find a way to resolve the issue sooner, but to no avail.

My friend helped me accept that we would be in Costa Rica for at least three more days, and suggested we turn the experience into an adventure. It gave me reason to use my new mantra, "does this add value to me life." I could have spent the weekend in fear, but instead, I chose to explore the city and create new memories. We enjoyed visiting malls, waiting for Ubers, dining out, and taking walks to discover various types of plants. It was a weekend of shedding the old and embracing the new.

On Monday, with my friend's assistance, we went to the Embassy and everything went smoothly; I was able to obtain an emergency passport to return home. We ended up sleeping in the airport, which I learned is quite common. I appreciated the excitement, and the learning experience this weekend provided. I believe that the healing I received from the retreat guided me through these events, and I truly enjoyed the experience. I am grateful to my friend for staying by my side throughout.

Several months after the retreat, while walking in my backyard and connecting with nature, I received a profound insight. A friend recognized my worth enough to dedicate her time to support me through my experience in Costa Rica. The disaster I perceived was seen by her as an opportunity for growth. Her actions have enabled me to reflect on my worthiness, especially during times of self-doubt. I can affirm that I am deserving of love and respect from my community. I no longer feel the need to conceal my family history or trauma; I am worthy today and every day.

Chapter 21

"Nobody will protect you from your suffering. You can't cry it away or eat it away or starve it away or walk it away or punch it away or even therapy it away. It's just there, and you have to survive it. You have to endure it. You have to live through it and love it and move on and be better for it and run as far as you can in the direction of your best and happiest dreams across the bridge that was built by your own desire to heal."

Cheryl Strayed

I am continuing therapy and learning to apply new insights, recognizing that my self-worth and energy are not dependent on others' opinions or what I can do for them. I am discovering my true identity, separate from the roles I have portrayed over the years. I have managed to slow down and let go of overwhelming tasks I previously imposed on myself. Reflecting on my journey with three different therapists, I see each as a necessary part of my healing process, each arriving at the right time in my life. I appreciate all three and the progress I have achieved.

My family of choice is my foundation and has supported me through all my therapy sessions, both positive and challenging, consistently reminding me of their unconditional love.

My relationship with God has evolved over the years. I once believed in a deity called Satan, then viewed God as angry and warlike, and later as a vague "Higher Power". At times, I considered God as insignificant, and at others, I kept an open mind about people's concepts of the divine. I felt compelled to earn His love to establish a relationship with Him and prioritized others' opinions over God's. Eventually, I began examining my trauma through psychological perspectives, gaining insight into how the brain functions. I now believe that God does not need to be an invisible entity I have never connected with but can be experienced as a guiding presence in nature, which I find to be perfect.

Understanding an artist can be achieved by examining their artwork, just as songwriters can be understood through their compositions. I strongly believe you can grow stronger to the Creator through His perfect Creation. I find peace in nature, appreciating its perfection and trusting it to guide me correctly. I have started to prioritize self-care, particularly nurturing my inner child, by asking myself before taking on responsibilities, "Does this add value to my life?"

Currently, I am engaged in a healing journey aimed at restoring my sense of wholeness. This process has been gradual, involving the incremental release of numerous traumatic memories that have shaped my past. Having a compassionate and supportive therapist has been essential in this journey. My therapist provides a safe space for me to express my emotions, including moments of intense distress or meltdowns, and she consistently demonstrates unwavering commitment to my growth. Her patience and understanding have been instrumental in helping me navigate complex trauma and break free from old, unhelpful patterns. As I progress, I recognize my inherent value and continue to build my self-esteem and inner strength through my relationship with God. This spiritual connection offers me additional support and guidance, reinforcing my resilience and fostering ongoing healing and self-discovery.

As a dedicated resource for individuals grappling with complex trauma, I am committed to sharing my personal journey of healing and resilience. Through a collection of heartfelt letters written to myself after therapy sessions, I aim to offer support and insight into the challenging process of confronting difficult memories and emotional struggles. These writings reflect the perseverance required to navigate trauma and the importance of self-compassion during recovery. I am profoundly grateful for the encouragement that motivated me to pursue healing. I know my experiences can inspire others to find their own path toward recovery and emotional well-being.

Therapy is not easy. My therapist has been steadfast in her commitment to me. When I go down self-destructive patterns, becoming dependent on her and other people for my self-worth, she gets me back on my path, reminding me I have the self-energy to depend on myself and my value. I get angry at her because she is not playing my games. After much self-reflection and my past patterns, I really want to find my self-energy, through my relationship with God and nature. My mind continues to believe I need attachment from my mom, or anyone, to provide my self-worth. My therapist has walked with me during all my destructive behaviors. She has never given up on me, although there were many times I wanted to quit. I attached some personal notes I wrote about hard therapy days to introduce to you to my trauma mind.

Journaling

Reflections on my counseling experiences

It was so difficult and so eye opening. Tons of insight for me.

I was too disgusting for my mom to ever touch me. No one is my mom.

I had touch from my support ladies at church. Do I pick the unhealthiness of the church over my need for validation?

People hurt me so bad and when I am dealing with that pain it would feel good to be nurtured rather than alone in that pain. I have a blanket over me so no one has to physically touch me.

I know my therapist is not my friend and I have been and will continue to work on it. I attach to anything and when I pull away to move from that unhealthy attachment, I am becoming distant feels like a double message all my life.

What is the therapist boundaries? Do I work on gut level never felt feelings with no validation?

If that is the case, I can do that well.

I feel so guarded in what I write. I am so, so
sad and can't stop crying. I realized today
that I have to do this through my own self-
energy. She (or anyone else) cannot do this for
me. I have to build my connection with myself
with the help of my God. She can't take away
my pain, she will not heal me, connect me to my
heart, nobody can do that except God. She knows
my patterns and under my pain, I know she is
right. Just been looking for the right person
or people to rescue me and I can only rescue me
with support from my community.

So many times I wanted to quit therapy because
of the pain involved but I hung in!

I did a lot of work at the fire. Much of my
pain involved fire. She came to me, and
comforted me. It was so much easier to pass
through that pain and I do not have that pain
anymore. That was something that worked for me
and that is why I say, someone I do not connect
with. I know my therapist is not my friend. I
do not want that anymore and I have come to
terms with that but please be my therapist. It
felt so good to roll through Rebecca like that
and it just took validating my feelings for me
to move forward. Maybe I got everything I need
from this therapist, but I don't feel in my
heart that it is completed.

As we went deeper into the pain of events I had never allowed anyone to see, therapy got harder for me. I started releasing anger, and my therapist took the brunt of it. When I felt unknown feelings, I did not know where to direct them, except to her. I guess we do that with people we feel safe with. I did not understand what I was feeling or how to handle such deep feelings. All I know is the pain hurt deep down. Coming to terms with what I was raised in and what was done to me became overwhelming. The horrific images and memories my brain had been holding on to began to come to the top. I freaked and made many acquisitions against people that loved me. I quit and came back to therapy so many times in my head. I processed a lot on paper after therapy because my mind was pretty occupied with images.

This has been the start to my deep inner healing.

Journaling

I have fallen to a weakling and I do not like needing things (touch) from people. Why does God have me here. Is it because I have grown away from him and this is my consequence? I spoke with a fellow counselor today using no names and was very honest with my needs. He helped me see I am looking for confirmation as the past event is happening. He really was caring and I felt no threat from him.

Why can' t I sleep? I have so much on my mind. I love my therapist to death as a therapist. She has brought me where no one has brought me before. I trust her more than I have trusted anyone on the level of pain I have gotten to. I love the way she doesn' t let me sit idle and pushes me through the pain. This is really tearing me up inside because I need her to continue pushing me through this. Did I totally screw up this therapy relationship? I cannot believe I am going to put this on paper but if I didn' t have responsibilities I would check into a hospital. That is very scary for me to acknowledge. Why am I a f..k up trying to figure all this out? My counselor friend made a suggestion. He told me about different modalities of therapists. Some are hands on, some are not. I really have been processing a suggestion he made about bringing a motherly figure with me to counseling. That sounds like

a quick answer to everything and he has seen it
work for people before. Of course, I would
bring my friend. She has been through trauma
herself, and understands the pain. I have know
her for 10+ years. She could sit next to me and
let me be angry at so many people who hurt me.
The men in my life. I know she would support me
hitting her and still be OK with me. I could
cry tears of sadness and she would comfort me.
It sounds like a really great plan and an answer
so I don't feel stuck. She said she will do it,
but do I really want her there? No, I don't
want to share that deepest level of pain with
anyone. I know she would have empathy for me,
but I don't need f..king empathy, I need
someone on the other side, someone to touch when
I feel disgusted and downright hating myself.

I stand there in so much pain and that cum stuff
all over me and they would touch me and tell me
I am important.

When those men come and someone to say you are
more important than this. When I feel angry
(very hard feeling) someone I can lash out to
but will build me back up to where I am strong.
I kinda feel my friend would "save" me and I
would put my worth in her rather than myself and
my ability to see that I am capable of doing
this. I know my patterns and my therapist
helped me see how this would not help me to move
forward but keep me stuck. I have shared with
my therapist my deepest pain in my heart and
she has built me up and showed me I can get this
from within instead of outside of myself, which

only has led me to disappointment in people. I want to finish strong with my therapist and not continue in my patterns of needing acceptance and approval from outside of me. Only God living within me can do this.

Journaling

I would like to not have the loyalty and vows of my family.

Release the bondage and the hope of being accepted by my mom, to stop trying to get acceptance from her, to let go of my soulmate. He really accepted me but scared me too.

To unite with my inner child

To be done with therapy

To go to Costa Rica

To let all of the guilt and burdens in my heart go

To have a different purpose in life than to be accepted

To not feel like I will be rejected by the people I care about

To find something I like to do for me

I feel like I have to get some attachment/closure before I can feel love

Me One year from now

Happy, laughing, outside activities

I would like to have a sharper brain and more space for good memories and useful knowledge

Purpose and vision for my life: something positive

Journaling

Tomorrow I see Noel again.   Not sure how I feel.
Haven't seen her in over a week.   Not sure if I
am ready to talk to her.   It's so easy for me
to move on from people.

It's hard because if I stop counseling now I
could do it and not feel anything.   But if I go
tomorrow I'll be back in my head.   I have been
having such headaches trying to keep it all in.

I feel so many mixed messages, come, go, come,
go, just tell me about your pain but I cannot
validate any pain that happened to you.   I need
to start praying for a strong woman that God
puts in my life that can minister to me in that
way.   Maybe that's why I called my friend when
Bree died, but it went straight into being wrong.
With my therapist, what I do is wrong so many
times.   I'm so tired of being wrong.   I know I
am a messed up person but I continue to try.
Maybe what I need is to find a therapist who
never had an attachment to anyone so they can
understand the pain in my heart.   I really have
come a long way with this therapist and really
want to continue with her.   I just need to do
better and understand her boundaries, which I
feel change a lot.

I did counseling today. Very anxious going in. I
felt like my therapist just wanted to keep
moving forward but really wanted to talk and

211

make a decision if this counseling relationship would work. I felt like I have split everything out but she still does not understand. I really felt today that I really want to heal so bad. I really want to get past this and I truly feel as if I can. I've got to get my life back together, focus on an invisible God who will fill me with his love me and accept me as I am. Everyone says this invisible God can heal me and I put my all in it for many years but could not bring him in me. I am so excited that God has shown me Gaia, Nature, totally sinless, created by him, that I am able to get my healing from. Nature was created in his image and is sinless. I find so much peace within her.

Why do I share my personal writings often written through tears? It is because I am on a journey toward embracing my authentic self. This process involves learning to love myself unconditionally, recognizing my worth, and understanding that this journey has been long and challenging. My hope is that others who are struggling can find hope and encouragement through my experiences, reminding them not to give up despite the pain and frustrations they face. Throughout this journey, I have come to realize that all the tears, frustrations, and personal growth are valuable and worthwhile. My therapist's guidance has been instrumental, and I have learned to trust the process, even when trust feels difficult, especially for someone who has experienced trauma. Trust is a fragile yet essential component of healing and overcoming the difficulty of trusting others and oneself has been a significant part of my recovery.

Today, I trust myself to make choices that add value to my life. This self-trust is a result of deliberate effort and self-awareness, as no one else can do this work for me. I am also healing my inner children, which is a metaphor for nurturing and caring for the vulnerable parts of myself that have been hurt in the past. This ongoing healing process is vital for achieving emotional well-being and self-acceptance.

Sharing my story is a way to connect with others who may feel isolated in their struggles. It serves as a reminder that healing is possible, and that perseverance through pain can lead to a more authentic and fulfilling life. My journey continues, but I am committed to embracing my true self and supporting others on their paths to healing and self-love.

Chapter 22

Before authoring this book, I attended a class that
explained the various components and protectors I
developed to cope with childhood trauma. Internal
Family Systems (IFS) is a trans-formative therapeutic
approach that views everyone as a complex system of
protective and wounded inner parts, all guided by a
central Self. This perspective recognizes that the mind
is inherently multiple, which is a beneficial aspect of
human psychology. Similar to a family, these inner
parts can be pushed from their healthy, valuable
states into extreme roles, often as a response to
trauma or stress.

The Self, present in everyone, is unalterable and
possesses innate healing capabilities. It serves as a
compassionate and wise core that can guide healing
processes. IFS is widely recognized as an evidence-
based psychotherapy that facilitates healing by

enabling individuals to access and nurture their inner parts. The approach emphasizes establishing a connection between the inner Self and these parts, fostering understanding, compassion, and integration. This process not only promotes internal harmony but also enhances external relationships by cultivating a sense of conceitedness and self-awareness. Through consistent practice, individuals can learn to listen to their inner voices, address unresolved wounds, and develop healthier internal dynamics, leading to overall emotional resilience and well-being.

After completing this course, I felt well-prepared to write my book, integrating all my inner parts and protectors by first seeking their permission. This process was instrumental in fostering inner trust, as it provided them with a sense of agency, which they previously lacked. Such an approach has significantly contributed to my emotional healing, allowing me to acknowledge and incorporate my healing journey into my writing. I have experienced substantial healing over time, and I now sense that I am on the verge of complete healing. This realization is both empowering and inspiring, marking an exciting phase in my personal growth and creative process.

 # Journaling

TO BE LOVED

The basics of IFS therapy

Validation is a very big part of IFS

A child needs a lot of validation and if they do not get it they will try to seek it now.

My child needs validation and stability

When I get validation today, I wish it would validate some of my inner child stuff.

GET IT OUT validation help others, give them a voice, speak truth, look at it on paper. Get it out of my head, stop self harm, learn to love me, understand me.

Integrate all parts of me!!

A collection of writings follow that reflect my journey of healing and personal growth, illustrating the progress I have made over time. The first journal writing is written by my protector, which emerged at a young age. I did not understand this whole concept but have been open to researching it. If I had processed a lot of the images I saw as a child, my brain would have shut down, as explained in the IFS definition, written about earlier. It makes sense to me know how God uses our mind to protect us from childhood trauma. This concept made a lot of sense to me and today I can process those images because of the support system that has been created. Before making any judgement about this, please research IFS – Internal Family Systems.

Journaling

Little girl, what can I do to help you? What is
the block?

You can help me by listening to me.

I am listening to you and want to help you but I
can' t get to you. I can' t hug you or touch
you and I don' t know how to explain it. You
think I wouldn' t take every opportunity to help
you feel safe. You believe I am purposefully
harming you. You think I don' t want to give
you everything you need, you think I' m ignoring
you. Well baby, you can believe what you want.
You know the Spirit of Suicide you feel I
protect your mind to keep that from happening.
You see the old homeless people living in tent
cities. I kept you from that. Your mind cannot
or will not let you go in your pain. What' s
best, Mental Health Crisis or death. To live or
die. I will not let your mind make you crazy.
I understand your pain. I feel the pain you are
in and I am trying to help you. Please
understand. I respect you for what you are doing.
Helping you heal. But I am really scared for
you, baby girl. I have been protecting your
brain for a long time.

I caught you early but allowing one opening I
feel like it will start snowballing and you
won' t be able to stop it.

Help her understand⋯

I have placed in your head that the pain you currently feel is about not having a family and connection but instead until you have the strength, a spiritual base, and someone you can trust, I will not let you remember the images you saw as a child. That would make you crazy, if you had no one to support you through this.

That has kept your brain alive. This is the most I can give you. This is why there is very little connection between you and your girl. I want to keep your brain whole. I have been doing this for many years and I know how to do it.

———— ✦ ◆ ✦ ————

I can feel healing happening within me. I feel a true freedom and spiritual connectedness. I have been up and down so many different paths, AA, Unitarian Church, Christian Counseling, Indian Spirituality, Emotional Coding, Religion, Wellness Retreats, Yoga, all have had something helpful for me in each, and has brought me closer to believing I am worthy to God. All of this has brought me to a Spirituality I can connect to. Nature, that God created as perfect.

 # Journaling

Dear Baby,

I am coming. I am learning how to touch you. I
  do not want to hurt you anymore. I am so so
  sorry for using you as a ghina pig. Getting
adult attention from your pain. I am going to
  learn how to treat you better. There was a
    teacher, Ms. Pentecost that loved me. I
remember her touch and I want to touch you like
  that. I'm really working for you baby, and I
will keep protecting you until I can reach you.

My Intention: To deliberately give the baby
              love and trust.

Fear of acknowledging I am a good person

Journaling

Sitting in the hospital waiting on a room in NICU. I watch my foster baby, at 5 pounds, tiny, tiny, as they work on her tiny body, trying to get blood to draw. Seeing the needle, the foreign object, and trying to get it in her tiny body. Third time holding her, soothing her, rubbing her little head. It's okay precious angel. I am here, just rest. Second guessing getting her help, somewhere safe. I can use my brain to get her help. I bring her to the hospital. I am going to save this baby, I think as I watch all the monitors. I can get her help. I have the power to do this today. I was watching her struggle, hurt and suffering, trying to get breath, and I got her help. Second guessing my decision. She had stopped eating, hip-cups, yawning, sneezing, all symptoms of withdraw. Happening fast for a 5 day old baby.

She will be okay. NG tube inserted, getting nutrition, morphine, getting more comfortable. Today I have control for this 5 pound baby. In a soft bed, I call her name and it soothes her. Got her to a safe place with nice people. She stopped crying when she heard my voice. Safe Baby, Alive. She could have **died but didn't.**

I was caring for this foster baby who is in the process of withdrawing from drugs. Thanks to our training in addiction, we were able to recognize the signs of withdrawal early. This enabled us to take appropriate action promptly, which contributed to the baby's well-being. The experience reinforced the importance of applying our knowledge and past experiences in real-life situations, providing a sense of fulfillment and confidence in our care giving role. Recognizing the challenges faced by children in such circumstances underscores the significance of specialized training and compassionate intervention in fostering recovery and stability for vulnerable children.

A lot of personal healing took place during this incident. A lot of introspect into my own past, knowing I survived and today have a feeling of I CAN HEAL!

I am currently in a Bible Study with a great group of ladies. It is called Devine Joy by Nicole Zasowski. To paraphrase a chapter that made a lot of sense to me. The focus was on Sarah, Abram's wife. Some of the nuggets I have gotten from this study so far are:

- I am realizing I trust a known lie rather than a promised truth (I am unworthy rather than I was made in God's image)

- Joy is a very vulnerable feeling (it can point me to God or away from God)
- With Joy, many of us (especially trauma survivors) do not celebrate Joy. I am waiting for the downfall or the other shoe to fall. I miss the celebration of Joy because I focus on "what's next". (Something will steal my joy so why be joyful?)
- I have the power in my life to redefine joy in my life. Looking at joy as something happy instead of waiting for it to be taken away.

I have come a long way and I am determined to be healed. So many people have poured into my life. My heart is not black anymore. Maybe grey but I see the red slowly coming back. I remain teachable and willing to try different avenues of healing. I can be in the worst pain today, I go into nature and God speaks to me. Unlike anywhere else, Nature has become my safe place, where it is just me and God, and I hear Him.

I go back to the saying, "What if I fall? Oh, but darling, what if you fly". Today I know that I have a strong tree of hope to land in.

Conclusion

I am contemplating the idea of flying. I feel my body and mind rejuvenating, guided by God to pursue growth and liberation on this journey. As my relationship with God strengthens and my peace and serenity in Nature evolves, I believe I am on the right path. I am 65 years old, and my time is not up. I want to live today. I continue to work on pain, I have worked through my patterns of sabotage with my therapist, I have my family and the greatest support group. And I can do this. I want to acknowledge anyone who can relate to any of my struggles. Keep going in healing, even when it gets tough. Don't quit but reach out for help. I'm pulling for you.

A Doorway for Those Who Wish to Reach Out

If these words have touched a familiar place in your heart, and you feel the quiet pull to share your story, to ask, to seek connection, or simply to be heard, know that the author welcomes you with open hands and a listening spirit. Her paths of connection are here, lit gently for anyone who wishes to reach out:

Website: www.rebeccabaker-author.com
Facebook: Rebecca Baker – Author
Instagram: @rebeccabakerauthor
Email: contact@rebeccabaker-author.com

May your journey forward be met with understanding, and may your voice find a place to rest.